GRAPHIC COMMUNICATION

APPLYING PRINCIPLES

GARY COLL

Prentice
Hall

Upper Saddle River, New Jersey 07458

Library of Congress Cataloging-in-Publication Data

Coll, Gary.

Graphic communication : applying principles / Gary Coll.

p. cm.

ISBN 0-13-030516-2

1. Computer graphics. 2. Visual communication. I. Title.

T385 .C5456 2002

302.2′22—dc21

2001021506

Executive Editor: Elizabeth Sugg
Managing Editor-Editorial: Judy Casillo
Production Editor: Linda Zuk, WordCrafters Editorial Services, Inc.
Production Liaison: Denise Brown
Director of Manufacturing and Production: Bruce Johnson
Managing Editor-Production: Mary Carnis
Manufacturing Buyer: Cathleen Petersen
Design Director: Cheryl Asherman
Senior Design Coordinator: Miguel Ortiz
Cover Design: Joe Sengotta
Marketing Manager: Tim Peyton
Editorial Assistant: Anita Rhodes
Composition: Publishers' Design and Production Services, Inc.
Printing and Binding: Banta, Harrisonburg, VA
Cover Printer: Banta, Harrisonburg, VA

Prentice-Hall International (UK) Limited, *London*
Prentice-Hall of Australia Pty. Limited, *Sydney*
Prentice-Hall Canada Inc., *Toronto*
Prentice-Hall Hispanoamericana, S.A., *Mexico*
Prentice-Hall of India Private Limited, *New Delhi*
Prentice-Hall of Japan, Inc., *Tokyo*
Prentice-Hall Singapore Pte. Ltd.
Editora Prentice-Hall do Brasil, Ltda., *Rio de Janeiro*

10 9 8 7 6 5 4 3 2 1

ISBN 0-13-030516-2

CONTENTS

INDEX OF TASKS

PREFACE

Perhaps a bit of background will be helpful to those using this guide. I developed and have taught for a number of years a graphic arts course in the department of journalism at the University of Wisconsin–Oshkosh. For a number of years, our department did not have a proper laboratory, and so I focused on fundamental principles of graphic communication rather than on production of finished materials. Students learned these principles, passed the course, and were graduated. Some of them became professional communicators. They drew on their knowledge of the principles learned in the class and became successful at their jobs. When computers and graphics-related programs came on the scene, these graduates found themselves in training sessions where they learned to use computers to apply the principles of graphic communication that they already knew. They also learned that computers offer new capabilities and different possibilities for effective communications, and some became skilled at using those new capabilities. Of course I have invited a number of my former students to return to share their experiences with current students, usually by using a computer and image projector in a laboratory setting. Visitors have typically outlined a problem they once faced and then demonstrated how they solved it. Such visits have been successful. However, one of the results has been increasingly strong pressure from my students to emphasize computer skills in the class. Students have been quite open in expressing their conviction that, only if they learn to use programs such as QuarkXPress, Adobe Photoshop and Adobe Illustrator, and others will they be able to move smoothly into their professional careers.

I am not unsympathetic to their argument, but I don't feel I can justify spending the time needed to do much more than introduce some of the more useful programs and comment briefly on their capabilities. Besides, each day I see numerous examples of poorly conceived and produced graphic communications efforts in any number of media. So I continue to prefer to keep my graphics classes focused on learning and applying the principles of good graphic communication. This guide is an attempt at compromise. It offers both realistic and simple exercises that help develop each student's computer abilities while at the same time presenting fundamental principles of good graphic communication. The simplicity of the assignments allows students to spend at least some time learning computer skills, but the level of computer expertise required is not high. Once the basics are learned, most students build on that base and become facile quickly.

I would like to acknowledge the following reviewers for their comments and assistance in the course of the development of this book: Shelly Dean, Department of Computer Science, Cumberland County College; Martin Greenwald, Ed.D., Department of Fine Arts, Montclair State University; and Anna Ursyn, Ph.D., Department of Visual Arts, University of Northern Colorado. I also wish to thank my wife, Elaine, for her helpful comments and unwavering support.

INTRODUCTION

This book of information and exercises is designed for graphic communicators in a variety of programs—communicators in such areas as marketing, communication, advertising, public relations, and journalism. In short, these are the types of programs whose graduates may be called upon in their careers to produce high-quality printed materials. And yet, many such learners are neither exposed to the information nor encouraged to develop the skills that will allow them to successfully meet such publication challenges. The exercises in this book lay out a number of problems that provide practice in turning well-written and edited verbal and visual copy into readable and attractive printed materials, including brochures, letterheads, business cards, signage, packaging materials, and even posters.

Many educational programs have acquired or developed advanced graphics laboratories filled with scanners and printers connected to computers which, in turn, are replete with programs that can do everything from simple word-processing to sophisticated composition and more. And these computers are increasingly connected to the World Wide Web so that students can learn to deal with that vast network.

Employers of graduates of such programs have come to expect that their newly hired employees have not only mastered a body of knowledge and learned to express themselves both verbally and visually, but have acquired design and layout skills and learned about typography and the use of color, as well some of the subtleties of paper selection, printing, and finishing. Communicators enrolled in these programs anticipate this pressure and increasingly demand to be taught the kinds of computer skills they imagine will be required of them upon completion of the class. Of course few training programs can afford to devote too much time to teaching proficiency in using a wide variety of hardware and software. As a result, many students become so impatient to learn that they jump right in, load a few of the easier to use programs, and begin to do graphics. Unfortunately, they typically fail to appreciate that computers and programs are no more than convenient tools, and that, like all tools, they have potential for good and bad use. The rule of the small boy and the hammer ("Give a small boy a hammer and everything he sees will need pounding") is especially pertinent here. It might be rephrased in this context to: "Give a beginning graphics learner a computer with a word-processing program, a file of clip art, and a basic desktop publishing program and everything he or she does will use as many capabilities of the computer and the programs as possible." Some results may be felicitous, but often they are not. Some may even be counterproductive. To compound the problem, using today's computers is not especially difficult, and poor-quality graphics can pour quickly from laser printers.

To further complicate matters, because they are focused so tightly on learning about computers and software programs, many learners don't take the time to learn principles of good typography and design. They listen to lectures and may read a textbook, but when it comes time to apply their knowledge, they rush to a computer and work harder on producing *something* than on producing good-quality creative graphic materials. In short, they tend to focus more on the software than on the problem they are trying to solve graphically. They often work until they have something on their monitor and then they begin to manipulate it endlessly—until they feel they have stumbled onto a good solution. They then print it, submit it, and go to the next task. In short, they do not allow themselves the time needed to think about the job and its content, the client and the client's need, or the printing variables so that a meaningful solution can emerge. Of course, the instructor must play a significant role in this process, and the exercises in this guide should allow virtually all instructors to participate successfully.

This collection of exercises attempts to recognize that both graphic communication and computer skills must be learned, but that the computer should never be permitted to become the central focus in a beginning graphics course. Students must be convinced early on that many societies got along quite well (and typographically beautifully) without computers in typesetting, layout, and design for more than 500 years. As recently as 200 years ago, there were only two communication media of any consequence: newspapers and books. Newspapers then were just beginning to use headlines, and books were set in one of only four or five different typefaces and sizes, with little or no graphic relief for their grayed-out pages. Even with such apparent limitations on printing and distribution, the voyages of discovery, the Renaissance, Protestant Reformation, the progress of science from Newton to Einstein, popular appreciation of religion and the arts, as well as the computer itself emerged and developed largely by means of the plain printed (or even handwritten) word on paper. The lesson is that progress is not solely a function of technology, but it is realized when people are encouraged to engage ideas. Of course computers play a large role in this process, but it is essential to know the underlying principles of using type, visual copy, color, and design. In addition, a keen reading of the intended audience of the communication and its intended purpose is necessary no matter what material or distribution medium is used. Good decisions that enhance the capability of a message to transfer meaning are lodged, not in a computer, but in the perceptive understanding of the task or problem at hand and in thorough contemplation and consideration of the means available to help perform that task. Only at the end of the process does technology become crucial.

The exercises in this book will help learners begin thinking about and practicing skills they need to produce printed material that engage audiences. Information that should be helpful in completion of the assignments is included in each section. The assignments are challenging for learners beginning to think about graphic presentations. This book is meant to be a convenient source of relatively realistic assignments that can engage learners in the types of thinking that will help them produce reasonably professional materials. Instructors who use it will want to integrate the exercises with readings in their assigned texts and use their own lectures and discussions to place all learners on solid footing in graphics. Each assignment has a number and a title and a statement of learning objectives. In each section the assignment is discussed and information necessary for completing it is set forth. In some cases, visual materials are included at the end of a section. It is a good idea for anyone using this guide to read the full assignment before getting down to the creative work. Spending a little time getting it right the first time can save a good deal of time and energy in the long run.

One of the features of this work is the incorporation of background information to help introduce each assignment. This type of information can help students learn that there are enduring principles of graphic communication and also that there is still plenty of opportunity for the evolution of graphic content and form.

One other feature is the personal relationship of exercise to student. Normally, when a graphic communicator is presented with a graphic problem to solve, he or she has to undertake and complete at least minimal research before proposing a solution. Most assignments in this work assume the student is simultaneously the client, the graphic communicator, and the content provider of the proposed publication. Most students have a pretty clear sense of who they believe themselves to be, and they are able to move quickly through the research stage of proposing graphic solutions to problems. Hence this book contains an autobiography assignment, a personal identification mark assignment, a personal stationery assignment, a résumé assignment, and so on. Assignments that are not personal in nature deal with subjects that most students are familiar with, including shopping malls, favorite beverages, television, money, and so on. The exercises proposed in the workbook are easily adaptable to particular situations. Users can easily alter the level of difficulty of any assignment. Of course, student-instructor interaction is necessary.

This book is meant to supplement a good textbook on graphic communication. I feel comfortable using any of them, although I supplement them in my own lectures, graphic materials, field trips, and speeches.

1 AUTOBIOGRAPHY ASSIGNMENT

OBJECTIVES

This assignment is the first in a sequence that will help you learn some of the elementary principles and practices of typography and design. The assignments in this autobiography sequence will provide you with ample opportunities to learn about and reflect upon the proper use of type and visual copy for a given assignment and on the possibilities of presenting your selections attractively in a layout space. Because many typographic and design conventions in the graphic arts arose within the context of book design, completing this assignment will help to ground you in many current principles of effective design used in a variety of publications. A benefit of this assignment is that it extends over a substantial amount of time, not unlike a good deal of the work you will be called upon to perform in your career. This means that you will have to maintain your focus and allocate time wisely in meeting the needs of the assignments. Components in the sequence include

- Writing a chapter of your autobiography

- Planning and preparing a title page for it

- Developing an effective page layout plan for the pages of your autobiography

- Planning and preparing an attractive book jacket, including an author's blurb and the book's spine.

TO HAND IN

- A six-page (minimum) chapter of your autobiography

- A working title for your autobiography along with a subtitle and chapter title.

ASSIGNMENT BACKGROUND

As with a good portion of the exercises suggested in this guide, this initial assignment is based on you, personally. It is your autobiography. The reason for basing assignments on you personally is to spare you from having to conduct research before beginning to prepare the materials. However, remember that the first job for a professional graphic communicator on assignment would be to conduct whatever research is necessary to thoroughly understand the problem he or she is trying to solve and the array of solutions possible. At least for now, the research step will not require much time at all.

There are, however, some important challenges posed by these assignments. For example, your understanding of yourself will eventually be revealed to others not only in the content of the words you write, but also in the typefaces you choose and in the size, shape, and layout scheme you choose for your pages. Many times this guide suggests that when you are faced with a graphic communication problem, you should look around to learn how others solved similar problems. However, you should not slavishly follow or copy the work of others; in some cases, to do so would raise ethical or legal questions. Instead, keep looking at similar efforts until you have a pretty fair idea of the possibilities, and then sit back and let your own fertile imagination do its work in suggesting a particular, effective solution to the problem at hand. In other words, don't copy what you find, but use those examples as a jumping-off point for your own creative impulses.

ASSIGNMENT

Part One. This first assignment requires you to write, edit, and submit a manuscript chapter of your autobiography. Pick a part of your life that you feel comfortable in telling. Use any word-processing program you are familiar with (Microsoft Word, Claris Works, etc.) and specify 12-point characters and a common typeface. (You might want to try Courier or Geneva to start.) Set the dimensions of your page at $8\frac{1}{2} \times 11$ inches and place margins of 1 inch all round the page. Begin writing and don't stop until you have at least six double-spaced pages.

When you have completed your writing, print out a hard copy and edit it carefully. Make corrections, and then submit a hard copy. Preserve a copy on disk or hard drive for use later. Make certain that the pages of your work have an identifying slugline, preferably appearing as a header, and a page number.

Part Two. Think about the following variables and suggest a solution to each. Make a hard copy of your solutions to hand in and preserve a copy on your disk, for use later.

- What is the working title of your autobiography?

- What is a good subtitle to flesh out the title?

- What is a suitable title for the chapter you've written?

A working title can be looked on as a focusing device. Working titles can sum up a grand idea in only a few words, and if they appear as headers on all pages of a manuscript, they also provide instantaneous identification. Subtitles are supplementary to titles in both content and size of type. Sometimes they can be plays on words that open up new dimensions of a work intended to excite further interest. Pay a bit of attention to how others have handled these common parts of a work, and then, after a period of thought and reflection, respond with your own creativity.

TOPICS FOR THOUGHT AND CONSIDERATION

What information would you include if you were called upon to write a short blurb, or statement, about yourself such as those very often placed on the inside back flap of virtually any trade book jacket? Blurbs usually contain information that offers authors an opportunity to establish their contextual relationship with the work; magazines commonly rely on them to establish the credibility of freelance authors.

Also be thinking about how you see yourself portrayed in a book jacket photograph that accompanies a blurb. Are you smiling or serious? Are you looking at the camera or to the side? Is it a formal portrait or did someone capture the true you in a candid? What are your surroundings? What are you wearing? Eventually you will have to scan an existing picture of yourself or have one taken. So be thinking of the image you would like to project. Finally, begin to visualize a design for a book jacket. Stroll through a bookstore or library and pull down a number of books to see how professionals solve book jacket problems. Pay attention to the types of art and the typography used on these important wrappers, as well as the colors, special effects, and so on. Look carefully at the books' spines to see how publishers handle them.

2 TRIM AND TYPE PAGES, MARGINS, CONSTANTS, AND MASTER PAGES

OBJECTIVES

Creating spaces to hold printed material—for book and magazine pages and spreads, bulletin boards, and posters—appears to be simple. However, doing it well consistently over a wide spectrum of media can be an extremely valuable skill for any graphic communicator. A good beginning to developing the skills needed to accomplish this is to become familiar with type, art, and page space. When you have made some basic decisions about these variables, creating a printed work becomes much simpler.

TO HAND IN

- At least four thumbnails of facing pages copied from autobiographies you find in a library, with page and margin dimensions clearly marked, and at least two thumbnails of chapter title pages

- At least two thumbnails of facing pages of your own autobiography, with page and margin dimensions clearly marked, and a thumbnail of a chapter opening page of your own autobiography

- A full-sized chapter opening page rough, with your copy in place

- A full-sized two-page grid of facing pages, with your copy in place.

ASSIGNMENT BACKGROUND

As with the development of any skill, learning and then practice are in order. Fortunately, there is a simple approach to creating useful and attractive spaces on which to display printed materials. First, layout spaces must be appropriate in size and shape for the presentation of their content, and they should not differ noticeably in size and shape from what audiences have come to expect from similar offerings, unless there is a good reason for the variance. Second, readability is usually the most important consideration for most printed material, and apportioning space for lines of type is an important readability variable. For example, if a page appears to be too full of type, it may scare off potential readers. Lines of type that are too wide may tax an otherwise interested reader. Finally, proper arrangement and framing of printed materials on a page can increase an audience's acceptance of them by helping to make them appear inviting.

Whenever you volunteer for or are assigned a specific communication problem, a solid first step is to pay attention to how others have solved similar problems. In the case of your autobiography, it will help you to stroll around the library's autobiography section, where recently published autobiographies can easily be found. Leaf through a few of them until you have a feel for how book publishers typically present autobiographies of famous and infamous persons. Are the designers of those books in agreement on the general approach they take to this type of literature? Take along a line gauge/pica pole/ruler and a few sheets of paper. Take down a few books from the shelves and measure their pages, margins, and blocks of copy. Record the measurements so you can refer to them later. Do not allow what you find in this first step of your research to dictate precisely your solution to your own problem. Use your findings as guides only; use your imagination and creativity in crafting your own solution to your problem. Of course, if you find that virtually all autobiographies on a library's shelves are, say, 6 × 9 inches, it would not pay to deviate too far from those dimensions without good reason.

As you are doing this basic research, ask yourself the following questions and record your answers.

- How big are the pages of the autobiographies?

- Is there a common size?

Open a few of the autobiographies to facing pages. When professionals look at a page of a book they actually see two pages represented on the single sheet. One of them, the *trim page*, is the size of the publication after all printing, folding, binding, and trimming has been completed. Within this page, inside the margins, is what is called the *type page* or *live area*. This is the area of the page where type set *en masse* (the text of the work) appears. Another way to look at it is that the type page is equal to the trim page minus the margins. An example of trim and type pages can be found at the end of this section. Although headers and footers, page numbers, and even ornaments may appear in the margins, the type page, inside the margins, contains the textual material of the work. The headers and footers and other material are *marginalia*; they appear in the margin and are not a part of the text proper.

As you look at the pages before you, answer the following questions:

- Are odd page numbers on left-hand or right-hand pages? Always? Is this true for magazines as well as books?

- How wide, in inches or picas, are the margins (left and right, top and bottom)? They often differ in size. How do they differ?

- How big are type blocks on the pages? How wide? How deep? How much, expressed as a percentage of available page space, is given over to type copy? What does that leave for white space?

Look at a few pages on which chapters begin.

- Are these pages different from the others?
- Do they have the word *chapter* on them?
- Is there a large numeral representing the chapter number? Is the number of the chapter written out?
- Are the chapters titled?
- Is the type block on this page larger, smaller, or about the same size as on the non-chapter-opening pages?
- Are there page numbers on the chapter opening pages?
- Is the first paragraph on a chapter opening page indented? How about the other paragraphs?
- Are there other elements or decorations on any of the pages?

Spend some time looking at the book jacket and its content. Note when the use of visual copy seems to be appropriate. Shuffle though the pages and note what types of things are printed on the pages at the beginning of the book and at the end. Is there any ornamentation?

If you keep your eyes open, you should come away from this research portion of the assignment with a pretty fair idea of how professionals assemble most autobiographies.

Now that you have a good deal of information about how books are put together, you need to have a means of recording it in a meaningful manner. *Thumbnail sketches*, or *thumbnails*, are helpful for this purpose because they offer both a means of recording and visualizing a good deal of information quickly and a way to experiment with concepts for placing words and art on paper. A thumbnail is a miniature version of your finished product in which all the elements are placed roughly on a miniature representation of a page. Because they are small in size and easy to produce, thumbnails allow you to explore a wide range of possibilities quickly and without the expense in time of having to produce complete or full-sized renderings of your ideas. You can make thumbnails any size you wish, but it seems efficient to make them about 16 to the $8\frac{1}{2} \times 11$ sheet, or three to the sheet if you would like to add more elements in greater detail. If you need to see facing pages, they, too, can be easily sketched in. You can easily represent type blocks with penciled-in parallel lines, titles and headlines with heavier squiggly lines, graphics with freeform shapes, and photographs with square shapes with a range of tones in them, perhaps showing vectors that will help lead the viewer's eye from the darker tones to the lighter. Examples of thumbnail sheets are found at the end of this section.

Thumbnails are a reasonable first step to take in creating virtually any finished work. After you've tried out a number of ideas and settled on the one or two that seem to work best, you can move along to a *rough*, which is a full-sized version of your solution to the problem. In a rough, the page elements are no longer merely sketched in, but are represented by full-sized and reasonably complete elements. The computer has made the production of roughs very easy. A rough may be followed by a comprehensive or a mechanical, in which page elements are exactly as they will appear in the finished printed work. At one time, a comprehensive was the equivalent of a camera-ready version of a job given to a printer for making film and plates preparatory to printing the work.

Of course the computer has significantly affected this formula. Roughs and finished layouts are so easy and cheap to produce on a computer that the progression from thumbnail to rough to comprehensive may seem to be outdated because one can easily produce a seemingly full-blown finished work with little effort. However, using thumbnails allows easy testing of ideas, and, perhaps more important, it slows down the process of movement toward a finished solution, thus forcing graphic communicators to consider the work in all of its permutations before finishing it and moving along to the next problem.

ASSIGNMENT   For the first part of this assignment, work on thumbnail sketches of book pages you have run across, drawing in margins, copy areas, display type, white space, and so on. Note page dimensions on the thumbnails. Hand in no fewer than four thumbnails.

When you have completed the thumbnails of the works of others, move along to creating several thumbnails for your own autobiography. How do you want the pages of your book to look? What elements will be placed on them and what effect are you trying to create with your autobiography? What size do you want the margins to be? It may help to look at the physical printed form of the autobiography (when it has been completed) as representing you personally. Probably you will want to establish an underlying impression of order. You want the pieces of the autobiography to hang together strongly, because you wish others to see the consistencies you observed in ordering it. The pages and their appearances then become a sort of a visible you. If they are confusing and haphazardly put together, that is how others will likely imagine you to be. If they are orderly, that orderliness will be reflected onto you. Of course, you will also want your pages to present an inviting appearance to browsers and to sustain readability for those who choose to continue. You may also want to present occasional surprises here and there, or break the rhythm many readers get into as they move from page to page. Perhaps you might use a bit of unusual typography, a slash of color, an illustration, or a piece of art. A few minutes spent thinking about such matters at this point can save time and will almost always result in a far better solution to virtually any problem. If you put elements on the page willy-nilly and then begin moving them around you will find yourself making an endless series of changes and alterations. So concentrate first. Be thinking, always.

When you have thought long enough and hard enough, commit your ideas to paper in the form of thumbnails, at least two thumbnails of facing pages, and at least one chapter opening page (a later exercise will focus on chapter opening pages). Remember that you will be recording elements on the pages, including copy blocks, page numbers, headers, footers, and initial letters. Remember that you can represent copy by drawing parallel lines that give the appearance of gray, display type with heavy, squiggly lines or with hastily worked letters in proportion, initial letters with bold strokes, and so on. Try a variety of arrangements.

When you feel you have a winner—that is, two facing pages that seem to make sense to you and one chapter opening page—make a full-size rough, either on the computer or drawn full-size on paper. A rough is a full-sized blueprint of the finished work. Hand in both thumbnails and roughs, with titles, copy, and page constants such as page numbers, headers, and footers in place. Use the copy you generated in the previous assignment for the rough.

Although this completes your assignment, you may want to take an extra step and create what PageMaker and QuarkXPress call master pages, either on a computer or by hand, using T-square and triangles. In a nutshell, master pages are templates, with page constants such as page numbers, headers and footers, illustrations and art, and margins all set in place (or at least with space for them marked off in the case of hand-drawn templates or dummy sheets). The beauty of building and using master pages is that when you have decided on the appearance of two facing pages you have answered virtually all questions anyone might want to ask about placement of elements, size of margins, and so on for all pages in the work. Learning how to make master pages on a computer and constructing dummy sheets is a worthwhile expenditure of your energy when you are working on multiple-page publications. Certainly if you have an eight-page publication, or even a four-page publication, you might profitably spend some time creating master pages. Their thoughtful creation and faithful use will add a good deal of consistency to the printed materials you produce.

ASSIGNMENT AIDS   Below and on the following pages you will find several examples of how you might go about creating your own pages of thumbnails. You can create them and store them in your computer and print them out as needed, or you can create one by hand and photocopy it enough times to see you through a number of assignments. Examples of both separate pages and facing pages for a publication are shown. Of course, you may make them any size you wish.

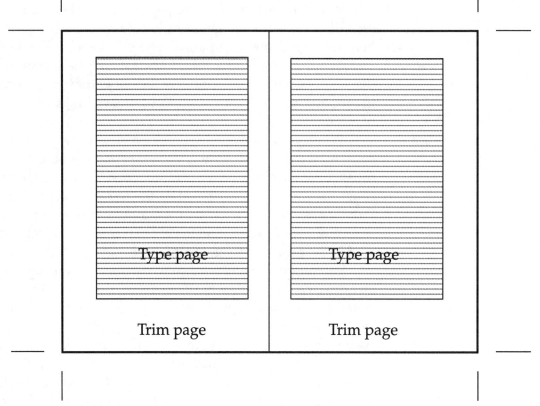

Trim page and type page with trim marks

Thumbnail sheet for separate pages, shown at 75 percent size

Thumbnail sheet for facing pages, shown at 75 percent size

3 MEASUREMENT IN THE GRAPHIC ARTS

OBJECTIVE   After completing this section of the workbook, you will be more aware of the variety of measurement systems currently in use by graphic communicators, and you will be able to measure type sizes and other elements. You will learn to use a pica pole to measure type and also begin to learn some of the vocabulary and skills used by graphic communicators.

TO HAND IN   There are a number of examples of type at the end of this section. Measure them and follow instructions for handing them in.

ASSIGNMENT BACKGROUND   Knowing how to measure elements in the graphic arts is extremely important, and knowing the systems commonly used to measure them is equally important. Each time you are asked to specify the size of a typeface, the width or depth of a page, or the width of a line of type, your success in being understood by others is based on how well you can apply one of a variety of common measurement systems. If you can apply two or three of them, you can make yourself understood virtually anywhere on the planet.

This was not always so. For a long while, measurement in the graphic arts was fairly informal. For several hundred years after Gutenberg developed his relatively cheap and effective means of casting type, each type founder was likely to have his own type measurement system as well as a personal vocabulary to refer to each type size in that system. Thus, typeface sizes and book page sizes bore names. Consequently, there were few standardized meanings agreed upon by everyone. Names used to describe sizes of type in one region did not always refer to the same sized type in a nearby town, much less in another region or nation. It was, at the very least, confusing. Because they lacked common measurement standards, printers and their clients found it difficult to work together efficiently, to say nothing of the difficulties experienced by press manufacturers and paper makers, who eventually came to realize that their profits could be maximized only to the extent that they mass-produced standardized products to sell to printers scattered all over the landscape. If you can imagine how handicapped everyone was by not being able to communicate precisely about their art and trade, you can appreciate the vision of such men as Pierre Fournier, François Didot, and others who devised clever and useful systems of measurement, some of which are used today.

A number of systems of measurement are currently in use in the United States, and although there will likely always be concerns about which is most useful and appropriate, the wisdom of Fournier and Didot stands out. In fact, an adaptation of Didot's system, called the *point system*, won official approval in the United States in the late 1800s and has been used ever since. It must be mastered by anyone serious about beginning a career in graphic communication.

This American system of measurement is based on the point, which is an arbitrary measurement representing a distance of about $1/72$ of an inch. Thus, there are 72 points in an inch. After this system came into general use, printers no longer were required to refer to type sizes by often imprecise names, but could identify sizes using a single number of points. The size of a piece of type was defined as the vertical dimension of a metal type body, top to bottom, necessary to accommodate all parts of all letters of the alphabet. Even with the point system in place, however, at least some of the original nomenclature hung on, and today two sizes of type commonly carry names: one is agate ($5\frac{1}{2}$ points) and the other is pica (12 points), both of which are shown.

This is a line of agate type

This is a line of pica type

Agate lines, or agates, were once the standard units for measuring national advertisements placed in newspapers. An agate line was one newspaper column wide and $5\frac{1}{2}$ points deep. Because newspapers no longer are the primary advertising medium for national advertisers, the word *agate* is now more likely to be used in a newspaper's newsroom to refer to the small type found on sports pages. Agate type, whether it measures exactly $5\frac{1}{2}$ points or not, is used to report box scores of athletic contests, bowling scores, and the scads of statistics of great interest to sports enthusiasts. *Pica* (12 points) may also be used in its original meaning to refer to a typeface that is 12 points in height, as measured from the top of the highest letter of the alphabet to the bottom of the letter that reaches farthest down.

Memorizing the following graphic facts will give you a good start on this important matter.

- One point is $1/72$ inch

- There are 12 points in a pica

- There are six picas in 1 inch

If the beginner learns to use only three units of measurement—the inch, point, and pica—he or she will be able to meet most challenges of measurement and will be well on the way to learning the common language of the graphic arts.

Each measurement unit is used for a particular purpose. For example, points are used primarily to measure and communicate about type sizes and the small amounts of space, called *leads* (*ledds*), that are often added between lines of type to enhance readability. Leading is most commonly a point or two. Using points to measure anything larger than type sizes and leading is not very practical because it would require dealing with large numbers. For example, a 6 × 9 inch page would have to be identified in points as 432 × 638. So, for page sizes, inches are preferred.

The pica (12 points) is commonly used to measure the length of lines of type (sometimes called the *measure*), the sizes of page margins, and alleys (the space between columns of type). Picas also can be used also to measure the size of art copy or even page sizes for books and periodicals.

Finally, inches are often favored for larger dimensions, such as paper sizes, trim page sizes, and so on. Inches can be used to indicate folding schemes for folders. Thus, a flat 8½ × 11 inch sheet can be folded twice to produce a piece approximately 3⅔ by 8½ inches. Sometimes newspapers refer to photographs as *x*-columns by *y*-inches. For example, a newspaper might identify the size of a particular photograph as a 2 × 5, meaning that its reproduction size will be two columns wide by 5 inches deep.

Those planning to work in graphic communication might also want to learn to use the metric measurement system. Although the point system is firmly entrenched in the United States, internationally the metric system is common. This means that the federal government and America's multinational corporations, including periodical publishers and advertising and public relations agencies, might eventually have to conform to this worldwide measurement system if they want to compete internationally. Most other nations have adopted the metric system and it can be confusing if more than one measurement system is used for a single printed piece, such as a periodical. Adobe Corporation selected a single metric trim page size for its *Adobe Magazine*, which circulated in both North America and Europe. By adopting metrics, Adobe simplified its page design process by having only one size for its U.S. and international editions. There was no need to design two separate publications because of subtle differences in size. The metric page is noticeably narrower and deeper than the U.S. standard size of 8½ × 11. *Adobe Magazine*, which is no longer published, was about 8¼ × 11¾, a size referred to as A4. The metric system also meets other needs, such as envelopes. Most U.S. paper companies have begun denominating their paper sizes in both inches and centimeters.

The system of measurement used by graphic communicators was never dominated by a single unit. Nor is it today. Proof is easily seen by looking closely at two of the more common composition programs, QuarkXPress and PageMaker. Both allow users to work in any one of a number of units of measurement, in addition to points. These include inches, inches decimal, picas, points, millimeters, centimeters, and ciceros (developed by Didot and still used in Europe). Although measurement in the graphic arts can be confusing, each graphic communicator should attempt to be conversant with the more common systems—points, inches, and metrics—and should learn to clearly specify which system he or she is using.

Although deciding whether to work in points, picas, metrics, or ciceros seems to be an abstract choice or one of convenience, selecting 9-point type instead of 12-point type produces real and significant differences in how typeset material is received by a potential audience. This seemingly simple choice between having eight lines of type in one column inch (72 points in an inch divided by 9 points per line) or six lines (72 divided by 12) might well mean the difference between a message sent and received and one that is sent but passed over unread because the space appears to be too congested or the type too crowded to be read easily. In order to make a reasonable decision on which measurement system to use and how many units to assign each element, the beginner should be familiar with the ways in which the systems are applied.

Type is commonly differentiated into two basic size groups. One, consisting of type one is likely to encounter while reading a newspaper or a book, is called either *body* or *text type*. It is type set *en masse* (in a substantial block or area). The primary function of type in this group of sizes is to get ideas across quickly, and a measure of their doing so is readability. Practically speaking, body type point sizes commonly range from as little as 6 or 7 points to perhaps 14 points, although most magazines use 10 point type, and many newspapers use 9½ point. These sizes are large enough to be easily seen and read but not so large that their message takes up an inordinate amount of space. Book and periodical publishers continually try to strike a balance between sizes that are readable and space considerations. Although 9.2-point type may bring complaints from readers that it is too small, 9.6-point type might calm critics by making it easier for some to read. The reverse situation might be the outcome if saving a bit of space is the most important consideration.

The second group of type sizes is called *display*. Headlines in newspapers, magazine article titles, and book chapter titles are set in display sizes. The functions of headlines and titles are numerous, but include shouting out a message as well as attracting attention by being large and heavy and also serving as a design element. The line dividing body and display sizes is more or less arbitrary and each publication comes to adopt whatever best meets its needs. Most graphic communicators focus on 16 points as a convenient dividing line between body type size and display type size. Type that is 16 points and larger is considered display type and is relied on to perform the functions assigned display sizes. Most computers allow a graphic communicator to select type from about 4 points to more than 100, in 0.1-point increments. Of course, it is difficult to argue that type varying in size by only 0.1 point is not really the same size.

When measuring elements on a page, the tool of choice is the line gauge or pica pole, one or more of which is on the desk of most professionals. A pica pole looks like a ruler and is marked off in inches along one edge and picas (12 points) and half-picas (6 points) on the other. Pica poles often are marked off with other helpful dimensions on their reverse sides (frequently in 8- and 10-point measurements). In addition to these scales, some pica poles have printed on them several capital *E*s in a variety of sizes from 6 points to more than 100. These examples allow users to estimate roughly the point size of type by comparing the sizes of the *E*s on the pica pole with capital letters of the typeset typeface in question.

Although in the long run a graphic communicator will develop his or her own means of determining an appropriate size for type in a variety of applications, measuring type as it appears in different contexts and mentally recording the results helps a beginner to develop a feeling for what size of type tends to appear in which contexts. Learning to use a pica pole aids in building confidence in performing a fundamental skill. In addition to learning how to measure type, beginners should use the pica pole to measure art copy, margins, page size, and other elements on a page or in a publication, as well as the size of the publication itself.

Most word-processing program users and desktop publishers are asked to specify typefaces and sizes and these selections are clearly displayed in a tool bar. However, the conventions of type measurement come from a much earlier time, before computers, when type was set in metal and when it had physical form, including letter height, width, and weight. (There are still type founders who cast letters in such form.) In those days, measuring metal type was a snap. A person just picked up a piece of type and held a pica pole next to it, measuring the size of the body of type on which the face appeared. The size of the type was, by convention, the size of the body of metal on which it rested.

Unfortunately, most type today does not have the physical form of a body of type, and measuring it calls for a bit more cleverness from the graphic communicator. To become clever, you have to learn to generalize from how type was once measured to how type generated in a word-processing or typesetting program, and which first appears on a monitor, is now measured. First, picture several metal pieces of type that make up the word *celery*, and then rotate them until you can look down on them.

Celery

Imagine several lines to which each character, letter, numeral, and punctuation mark relate. The lines have names and are used as guides by typographers when they develop new typefaces. Refer to the visual aids at the end of this section to help you draw in and label the lines.

- The *baseline* is the imaginary line on which the characters rest.

- The *x-height line*, or *mean line*, is the line to which many characters rise from the baseline, but go no higher (*a c e m n o r s u v w x z*).

- The *ascender line* defines the height to which some characters rise (*b d f h k l t*). Although capitals appear to rise to this line, typeface designers might choose to recognize a cap line, which is a bit lower than the ascender line.

- The *descender line* defines the low point on the type body to which some characters descend (*g j p q y*).

- A *cap line*, if used, is the line to which the capital letters reach. The cap line is usually a bit lower than the ascender line. The imposing bulk of capital letters seems to give them an added dimension. If they were to reach to the ascender line, they would dominate any line of type and would appear to be out of place and not the proper size.

- The *shoulder* is a small amount of space placed to prevent ascenders from the line below from touching descenders from the line above.

A graphic communicator who works with type soon comes to see that measuring display sizes presents few difficulties. If one has a pica pole with the capital *E*s included on it, it is easy to compare the size of capital letters of the typeface in question with the known size of one of the capital *E*s on the pica pole. If you don't have that feature on your pica pole, a second approach is to approximate the size of the type at hand by measuring the distance between the ascender line and the descender line, and then adding a small amount to account for the shoulder. Either method requires a bit of guesstimating, but neither is difficult and each yields fairly reliable results. An example of how each method can be applied can be found at the end of this section.

In the case of type set in columns, or *en masse*, the approach is a little bit different. One good approach is to mark off an inch of the column's depth (column inch), count the number of lines in that inch, and then divide the number of lines in the inch into 72 points. The result is the approximate type size. For example, if a 1-inch depth of a column in a newspaper contains six lines, you can assume that the type is about 12 point ($6 \times 12 = 72$). Leading can complicate this, but again one can usually get a rough approximation of type size by lining off an inch and counting lines. After a few times, you will feel pretty confident estimating type sizes, and you might even begin to ask yourself whether leading was used or not. Do this enough times with a variety of types and sizes in a variety of publications, and you will develop the knowledge that will help you to know which type sizes are appropriate or necessary in a particular application. From that point, it is trial and error; the beginner makes an informed choice, analyzes the choice when it is seen in print, and assesses the effect. If it was a good one, a little more learning has taken place. If the choice was not a good one, learning has also taken place.

ASSIGNMENT   Try your hand at measuring the examples below. Use points as your unit of measurement, and write your answer next to each example. When you have completed your measurements, copy the pages on which you did your work and submit the copies. Remember to look at the aids at the end of this section, where you will find several examples illustrating how you might go about measuring display type and type set *en masse*.

Opening Day includes Assembly

UW Oshkosh ranked tops

11 new classified employees hired

Budget goes
to assembly

Haupt storms square for WNA

UW-Oshkosh has been ranked among the top nine public universities in the Midwest by the U.S. News & World Report. It is the fourth year in a row that the magazine has ranked the school among the top public schools in the Midwest.

"This latest ranking reaffirms our continuing excellence among Midwestern public universities," said Chancellor John E. Kerrigan.

UW-Oshkosh has been ranked among the top nine public universities in the Midwest by the *U.S. News & World Report*. It is the fourth year in a row that the magazine has ranked the school among the top public schools in the Midwest.

"This latest ranking reaffirms our continuing excellence among Midwestern public universities," said Chancellor John E. Kerrigan.

UW-Oshkosh has been ranked among the top nine public universities in the Midwest by the *U.S. News & World Report*. It is the fourth year in a row that the magazine has ranked the school among the top public schools in the Midwest.

"This latest ranking reaffirms our continuing excellence among Midwestern public universities," said Chancellor John E. Kerrigan.

UW-Oshkosh has been ranked among the top nine public universities in the Midwest by the *U.S. News & World Report*. It is the fourth year in a row that the magazine has ranked the school among the top public schools in the Midwest. "This latest ranking reaffirms our continuing excellence among Midwestern public universities," said Chancellor John E. Kerrigan.

Ascender line
Cap line
Mean line

Baseline
Descender line

Above:
Measuring from the ascender line to the descender line (think points) and mentally adding a point ot two to account for the shoulder of the type should result in a pretty good guesstimate of the size of the type.

Below:
Lining off a column inch (72 points), counting the number of lines that are contained in that inch and then dividing 72 points by the the number of lines in a column inch should result in a pretty good guesstimate of the size of the type. In the result below, 72 points (the distance from line A to line B) divided by six lines equals about 12 point type.

A

When ideas compete in the market for acceptance, full and free discussion [exposes] the false and they gain few adherents. Full and free discussion even of ideas we hate encourages the testing of our own prejudices and preconceptions.

B

Full and free discussion keeps a society from becoming stagnant and unprepared for the stresses and strains that work to tear all civilizations apart.

Measuring display type and type set en masse

4 TYPE AND ESTABLISHING A TYPE POLICY FOR YOUR AUTOBIOGRAPHY

OBJECTIVES This assignment suggests a useful system of type identification, discusses some basic principles of typography, and introduces some of the vocabulary typographers use. This assignment will help you to become familiar with some of the varieties of type available to you, and you will begin to understand how type can be used to enhance messages and make it easier for you to communicate effectively with an audience. You will realize, too, that although type may have visual appeal or even emotional appeal, selecting the appropriate type for any particular purpose is an intellectual matter.

TO HAND IN You will hand in:

- Pasted up examples of eight type races or groups as well as examples of the family branches most commonly used

- Type specifications for your autobiography, based on library research.

ASSIGNMENT BACKGROUND *Races, Families, and Family Branches of Type.* More often than you would think, the choice of a typeface by a graphic communicator goes a long way toward determining the success or failure of a graphic communication. Good choices can attract attention, reinforce the content of a message, or make it easier to read. Good typographers do not often wish to challenge an audience and run the risk of having a typeface interfere with the audience's reception of their intended message. Instead they wish to accomplish the almost impossible task of selecting a typeface that will accomplish its intended purpose but which, in most instances, will not even register in the consciousness of readers. Knowing which type to select and how to present it is one of the more valuable skills a beginning graphic communicator can possess. And yet, typography, with its long and glorious history, is a subject so vast that to tell it would be nearly impossible, and to learn it completely so consuming that graphic communicators would have time for little else in their lifetimes. There are thousands of different typefaces, and if graphic communicators had to pore over the whole array each time they faced a choice, nothing would ever be produced. And yet there is ample evidence that graphic communicators make good choices of type every day and in a wide variety of contexts. How they accomplish that is a reasonable concern for beginning graphic communicators.

Choosing an appropriate typeface is possible in large part because most typefaces can be easily organized into a limited number of categories. Each category can be identified as performing a specific type of task well. So, graphic communicators do not really face the impossible task of picking a specific typeface from among the thousands available. They proceed by identifying a category of type that is likely to solve the problem at hand, and then they select a specific typeface from that category, based on their experience and knowledge.

Without venturing too deeply into the history and development of type, even a beginning graphic communicator can improve his or her chance of selecting an appropriate typeface for any given assignment by knowing a little bit about how the vast array of typefaces now available came to be produced and how past masters at typography solved typographical problems. That, coupled with a thorough and keen analysis of the job at hand, will greatly improve your chances of becoming a pretty fair graphic communicator.

At a minimum, a beginning typographer should be aware that for a long period, between 400 A.D. and the 1600s, books were about the only communication medium in Europe, other than oral. Their content was often religious, and they were produced by scribes in monasteries, who relied on a single agreed upon form for each letter of the alphabet (actually two forms if they used capital and lower-case letterforms). There were individual variations in form, depending on the tools used to create letters, and variations adopted in geographical regions. But, in general, people learned to read scribed letterforms even with these variations. Of course, the people referred to here tended to be better educated and were elites in the church and in secular society.

When Gutenberg came on the scene, it was entirely natural that he too would tend toward the printing of books, and that he would use as models for his letters the forms people already knew. There was relatively little dislocation in style or form of the alphabet as scribal communication gave way to printed communication, other than protests by scribes, many of whom eventually went to work for printers. But one of the enormous consequences of Gutenberg's work, and the work of printers who followed, was a general increase in literacy in the population, owed in part to cheaper printing. Credit for this democratization of literacy is also owed to Martin Luther, who arranged for the Bible to be printed in the language of the people rather than in Latin, and for giving common people an incentive to read the words of God for themselves. Cheaper and cheaper printing fueled more widespread literacy which, in turn, fueled demand for more printed works. And for a long while, demand for printed materials ran ahead of the supply. In this sellers' market, there was little incentive for innovation in typefaces and spatial arrangement of pages, or even in media. There was little need for style or graphic power. Whatever was produced found a ready market.

But gradually technological developments related to printing and the continual extension of education to those in society not already literate changed the situation. At some time in the 1800s printers found themselves capable of printing more material than people thought they could absorb. In this buyers' market, the concern shifted from meeting to creating demand. For anyone in the market, the problem became one of calling attention to his or her particular message, which might be one of hundreds or thousands competing for attention. A flurry of creativity in typography resulted as printers tried to draw attention to their own print list by differentiating their work from that of others. Because by then the size and format of printed materials was fairly well agreed upon by paper companies, press manufacturers, and the length of readers' arms, competition for attention turned to developing new attention-getting typefaces. By the end of the first quarter of the nineteenth century, the original several dozen tried and true typefaces that had served book publishing for more than 300 years had been augmented by hundreds of new type designs, some quite ugly and grotesque, some beautiful and graceful.

Gradually, the availability of an increasing variety of typefaces forced some to think seriously about how type and typography could be rationalized and harnessed to meet new needs. Part of the solution was to organize types, apportioning them into meaningful categories based on their characteristics, which could be related to their uses. Many suggestions were put forth, but one of the best is a modern scheme, by Alexander Lawson. He assigned types to one of eight races:

- Blackletter

- Oldstyle Roman

- Modern Roman

- Transitional Roman

- Square serifs

- Sans serifs

- Scripts and cursives

- Decoratives and novelties

Although knowing that types in the Roman Oldstyle and Roman Transitional races tend to be the most readable is helpful, it is not sufficient to merely specify a race when selecting a particular type. Races are broad categories, each with many members. Types are usually specified by their family name. Types in a family, like members of a human family, share many if not all of the specific characteristics that differentiate them from other families. Often the family name derives from the name of the person who created the specific typeface, as in Caslon, Garamond, Cooper, Bodoni, and so on.

Further, also as in human families, there are family branches of types, that is, types that share the same characteristics of appearance as others in the family, but that differ on one of several variables. For example, types can appear upright or perpendicular or slanted, or as typographers would say, perpendicular or italicized. Other family branches are based on the degree of boldness of the strokes that make up the typeface or the degree of compression or extension of the individual characters along a line. There is a scale of boldness, ranging from light through full face or regular to bold, extra-bold, and even ultra-bold. The range of extension goes from condensed through full face or regular to expanded or extended.

𝕭lackletter (Old English Text MT)

The first types to be cast in metal were modeled after the types of the time, the scribal Germanic forms, which were drawn with a goose quill pen. They tend to look angular, noncurving, and austere. They are sometimes called *text*, from the Italian *textura* (woven) because of their pronounced vertical appearance. All in all, they are not very readable and today we do not see much of them. They remain useful in limited ways, finding major use in church-related work, in secular venues for official certificates and diplomas, and in some newspaper nameplates, including *The New York Times*.

Roman Oldstyle (Caslon Openface BT Regular)

Knowledge of printing and typecasting came to Italy when some German printers crossed the border and set up shop. In Italy, they saw examples of the Latin alphabet carved in stone everywhere. These letters were curved and graceful and contrasted starkly with blackletter, and typecasters rushed to incorporate some of their best features in new typefaces. Much of the best and most enduringly beautiful printing of all time came out of Italy in the next few hundred years, and Roman type was its strength. Roman faces were designed and refined many times over under pressure of reader needs. Their strength was that they were exceedingly readable, generally because of three properties all three subraces of Roman types have in common. They all have serifs, they all exhibit what might be called an angle of emphasis or angle of stress, and they all have variations of a greater or lesser degree in the thickness of the strokes that form letters. The specific way each of these variables is handled determines whether a typeface will be assigned to the oldstyle, modern, or transitional race.

Claude Garamond was an early designer of oldstyle type, and the face named after him is still used today. His serifs are bracketed or swept into the main strokes and there is a pronounced diagonal stress to the letters. And, because the printing of the time was accomplished under difficult conditions, the overall weight of the letters tended toward heaviness. Thus, there is not a great deal of stroke variation. So, they can be recognized by:

- Serifs that are bracketed

- A pronounced diagonal angle of stress

- Relatively equal strokes

Other popular families in the race are Jenson, Goudy, Kennerly, and Caslon.

Roman Modern (Bodoni MT Ultra Bold)

This is also a Roman race, so we would expect there to be serifs, differences in strokes, and a pronounced stress. We find all three, but in different measure from oldstyle. The archetypal modern face is Bodoni. When Giambattista Bodoni developed his typeface, he was becoming concerned with meeting the typographical needs of the emerging commercial markets and attracting attention to new ideas and new products. And so he sent his types into the field dressed differently enough from oldstyle to attract attention. Because he printed on a relatively smooth, high-quality paper, on an improved press, with better inking, he could and did take liberties. His types have a pronounced vertical stress (imitative of the pen handwriting of the time), the serifs have been reduced to hairlines, and there is a good deal of variation in stroke weight between the thickest and thinnest parts of letters. The price of recognition and the elegance of modern type is exacted from its readability. These types tend to be more easily seen than read. Bodoni also developed a variety of borders, rules, and other typographical devices to complement his types.

Roman Transitional (Times New Roman)

The word *transitional* refers to a style rather than to a time period between the appearance of oldstyle and modern races. The indicators of this race are its stronger stroke contrast (but not as much as modern) and straighter, sharper serifs (but not hairline) than oldstyle. John Baskerville was the leader in their development, even though he was an amateur printer. He had access to tools and technology that allowed him still more freedom than Bodoni had enjoyed. He used it to produce a strikingly readable and beautiful typeface which was named Baskerville. In the early 1900s a group of faces of this race were designed to do specific work in periodical publishing. By the 1900s there were some popular magazines with circulations so great that they required high-speed presses to complete their press runs in good time. The need for fast printing coupled with a concern for readability led to the development of a subrace of transitional types that might be called *readability faces*. They are a little bit on the heavy side, as are their serifs, because they needed to stand up to a good deal of punishment on the press. They also have some readability features such as a large *x*-height and openness of letters. Many of them took the names of the publication for which they were designed. One of the more popular designs was Stanley Morrison's Times Roman, developed for *The Times of London* newspaper, later succeeded by Scotch Roman, then English Times and New English Times. Others of this readable and popular group were Century Schoolbook and Bookman, types used in *Century* and *Bookman* magazines and in textbooks for the young. These types came to be models for those who took readability seriously. Use of the words *schoolbook* or *bookman* in the name are giveaways.

Square Serifs (Geoslab Lt BT Light)

These types have serifs, but they are the same weight as the strokes, giving faces within this race a uniform weight and imposing appearance. Perhaps because of the craze for things Egyptian at around the time of their emerging popularity, some of them were given Egyptian-related names, such Memphis and Karnak. There is also the story that ties them to Napoleon's army, which is said to have used models of them for communicating by sign over great distances, because the letters were hefty. Originally they appeared only in capital letters, but lower case eventually evolved. Also, over time, their serifs have been treated in a variety of ways; one of the best recognized faces, called P.T. Barnum, has tall serifs and is almost universally recognized as "circus type." Other good examples are Stymie and Clarendon. They have proved themselves to be good advertising faces.

Sans Serifs (Futura)

These types have no serifs and tend to have no variation in thickness of their strokes. They generally are assumed to be a typographical response to the Industrial Revolution because they seem to be created by stripping away serifs and converting to a monotonous single-stroke weight, as a machine might require. They are extremely simple in appearance, and they tend to be easily picked out, which makes them good for display. Stop signs make use of them, as do many advertisements and signs. Many newspapers use them for headlines to contrast to their Roman faces, thus providing variety. Lately, some varieties have been adapted to readability needs with little serif bulges and stroke variations. Good examples are Futura, Franklin Gothic, Helvetica, and Optima.

Scripts or Cursives (Ribbon)

These types imitate handwriting and tend to carry the idea of both formal and informal equally well. They are definitely feminine and are considered stylish and elegant. They are unreadable in all caps.

Decorative or Novelty (Sand)

This is a catch-all category. Decoratives tend to be types jazzed up. Novelty types tend to be formed to create associations in the reader's mind with an idea or product.

The family branches most commonly used, and which you are asked to find and label, include:

italic or oblique

boldface

extra or ultra-bold

condensed

expanded

As you learn more about type and typography, it is likely that you will find yourself confused from time to time, especially if you find an example that has characteristics of two races. Perhaps you will find what you judge to be a square-serif typeface in which the serifs are so unusually large that they remind you of a type often appearing on circus posters, causing you want to place it in the decorative and novelty race. Or you might run into an especially flowing Roman italic that you feel is almost script or cursive in appearance. Or you might even find a sans serif type that seems almost to have serifs, or at least little hints of them, at the ends of stems. To find such things is not uncommon, and you can learn to deal with them. Remember that the reason for learning the main characteristics of the races is to work out a scheme for using them appropriately, and not to participate in an endless exercise of categorizing. Ideally, you will want to uncover underlying schemes for how particular types can be used. If you can, it may help to imagine what might have been going on in the mind of the graphic communicator who used them.

Type Policy. Learning about type is not an empty exercise. Everyone who publishes printed or even Web-based materials has to think carefully about typeface choices. The outcome of this sort of reflection and experiment is a type policy for your work. Deciding on a type policy involves selecting the races of type, families and family branches, as well as the sizes of type that you will use to get your message across to your audience(s). A type policy is nothing more or less than a well-thought-out and complete list of the typographical choices you identify as necessary to communicate your message effectively. It is complicated only to the extent that you have to be aware of all of the conceivable types of content in a work such as your autobiography that you wish to differentiate typographically from one another. You already know that type can be divided by size into display and text type, and that the function of display type is to attract attention to itself for some purpose or another, and that the function of body copy is to invite and sustain readability. You also know the races of type that can be used to facilitate readability, those with extra potential to be visible to a roving eye, or those that might enhance or reinforce your message.

Again, a good approach to learning about making such selections might be to wander through a library picking out autobiographies at random and examining them to see if you can derive a type policy for each. Note all of the uses of nondisplay or text sizes of type. To help you get started, note that a book's title page likely includes the title, subtitle, author's name, and publisher's information. This page alone might represent three or four decisions on face and size. Then there are other pages in the frontmatter of the book (copyright page, acknowledgments page, and so on) as well as some in the backmatter (appendices, indices, and so on). Chapter titles (if they are used) probably will be in display sizes. You may also find subheads in the text, or initial letters. Then there are body sizes, including the text itself and page numbers. If there is art, there may be captions and cutlines. Do your best to identify the varied functions you will want type to perform and then decide on type families and branches, sizes, and so on that seem to you to best perform those functions.

When developing a type policy for the first time, it is important for a beginner to understand that although there are thousands of different-appearing typefaces, this doesn't necessarily mean that a different one has to be identified for each particular use. Although it seemingly flies in the face of all reason (why would there be thousands of types available if we weren't meant to use them?), you might profitably begin by selecting a single face for a work such as an autobiography. Although this approach does not seem very exciting, adopting it can lend an impressive degree of continuity to the work.

This single-typeface approach is not as limiting as you may think, because you can differentiate a single face by varying its size, family branches (degree of boldness and extension and posture), capitalization schemes, and even color to differentiate your wishes for how the type is to be used. You can also incorporate rules and borders for good effect. There will be plenty of combinations available to insure that the single-face approach will work well.

Of course, sometimes you will want to mix typefaces. The trick is to know when this is indicated. The use of more than one typeface in a single work can generate typographic excitement. But if you decide to mix type on a page, make certain the faces are truly different. If they are not, that can easily confuse a visitor to your work. So, for example, you might be successful using a Roman oldstyle and a sans serif (which are clearly different in structure), but not if you mix a Roman oldstyle with a Roman modern (which have very similar structures). Although it generally requires typographic sophistication to mix type well, don't shy away from the attempt. Just think carefully about the problem, identify possible solutions, select the best one, and then look for and carefully analyze any feedback you receive on the attempt. It might be fruitful for you to accumulate an assortment of examples of how professionals have solved such mixing problems and look through them from time to time to familiarize yourself with solid possibilities. Use a copier to create the entries for such a file.

Roman Oldstyle/Roman Transitional (Both are Roman and have many characteristics in common. This mix may do more to confuse readers than allow the graphic communicator to make much of a typographic statement.)

Roman Oldstyle/Sans Serif (These are from races different enough to allow them to work together well.)

A type policy should be established whenever a graphic communicator begins work on a book or periodical, and developing one should be strongly considered even for occasional or one-time productions (ephemera) such as booklets and folders. In arriving at an informed decision, you will want to consider the following:

- The work itself (maybe a blackletter for an invitation to a medieval-theme costume party, or a script for a wedding announcement).

- The audience and its capabilities (very young and very old persons might have difficulties with type that has a good deal of intricate ornamentation or one whose letters are difficult to distinguish one from another).

- Your client, the client's budget, the printing process and so on.

Graphic communicators often develop type favorites and become comfortable using them, or they turn to trendy types that beg to be used because they are hot at the moment. There are several good ways to learn about which typefaces might be good to use. One is to look on the back pages in the books of some publishers, especially Knopf. Knopf has become known for identifying the types used to set the textual matter of its books, and often the type's history and development are included. Also, as periodicals engage in facelifts, they very often make typeface changes, and then tell their readers about their new looks. Frequently they discuss families and type sizes they plan to rely on and may hint at reasons for the change. Keep your eyes open to choices others have made and learn from them.

As you develop your autobiography type policy, consider the content. Is its underlying or persistent theme serious or upbeat, humorous or sad, ironic or comical? Type families often exhibit a good deal of character, and if you can match the character of the face with the character of the content, the whole thing sort of feeds on itself and becomes much more effective. You can sometimes create a cumulative or even exponential effect if you make a felicitous choice.

Big and ⊤**all**　　　　a **l o n g** time

In warning, this kind of effect can be accomplished much more readily on a cover or book jacket and in display type sizes rather than in the body of the work. You can try to be clever with a cover, but generally you don't want to attempt to sustain cleverness over several hundred pages of text. Generally, the work of the book's insides is to present ideas in readable typefaces that do not have intrusive characteristics that can stand in the way of promoting the rhythmic eye movements that a good readable type can establish.

ASSIGNMENT　　Hand in pasted-up examples of the eight type races or groups discussed here as well as examples of the family branches most commonly used. You will easily be able to find examples in periodicals and newspapers. Either copy and label each of your examples, or cut out the example, paste it on a sheet, and label it.

Also hand in a type policy for your autobiography based on your library research and on your reflection upon your work.

5 FINDING AND USING THE OPTICAL CENTER, PROGRESSIVE MARGINS, MARKING UP TYPE

OBJECTIVE

This assignment will help you to appreciate how placement of elements on a page can enhance your printed messages. Clever use of space, including placement of margins, establishing a typographic hierarchy, and adding the concept of typographic pacing can help a reader process information.

TO HAND IN

- A single book page with your name at the optical center of the page

- Two examples of how a title can be broken into either two lines or three

- An example of a title page, with title, subtitle, author's name, and publisher's name appropriately placed.

ASSIGNMENT BACKGROUND

Optical Center. That point on a page to which a reader's eye is drawn is without question the most important part of the layout. The single most important idea the graphic communicator wishes to express in the layout should appear there. This point in the layout is also often where a graphic communicator wants the reader's information processing to begin. Placing a meaningful graphic element where an audience member usually begins to process information can strongly determine the frame of reference within which the overall message will be interpreted. For example, if the first elements the viewer sees are light, lively, colorful, and upbeat symbols (such as a smiling clown's face), the viewer's frame of reference for processing the message will tend to be upbeat. If the symbols and images appear to be serious and somber (a graveyard scene), that can help create a wholly different frame of reference in the mind of a receiver of a message. Clever graphic designers want to control entry to the page in order to take charge of the frame of reference and also establish the path the reader will take through the layout. Knowing how to encourage a reader to begin at a particular point on the page, augmented by a clever use of space and the establishment of an appropriate typographic hierarchy, can help a graphic communicator get meaning across quickly and effectively.

Unfortunately, there is no single rule that tells a beginner where each and every reader will choose to enter every layout. There are, however, some general principles that most graphic communicators follow most of the time to attract the viewer's eye to this place of importance. One of the more dramatic means of attracting attention is to place a strong graphic element at the appropriate spot in the layout. This element and its page location then become a focal point, because they scream for attention. Such a focal point can be created from such elements as visual copy (preferably with striking content), heavy textures, unusual typographic treatments, enlarged elements, color, and so on. It is a "build it and they will come" proposition. The graphic communicator selects an important element and decides upon a special (and appropriate) graphic treatment, applies that treatment as strongly as he or she dares, places it appropriately within the layout, and readers' eyes will be drawn to it.

Another influence on the reader's eye is not so dramatic, but affects where a viewer's eye begins its journey around a page. This influential spot on the page is the *optical center*. It is the place on a page where, all other things being equal, readers' eyes tend to land, and where they (in cooperation with the viewer's brain) begin processing the message. The idea of "all other things being equal" means that if a designer has not consciously created a strong and attractive focal point by dramatically placing or treating an element, and if nothing in the layout stands out or is particularly dominant, a reader's eye will generally begin the work of interpreting the message at or near the optical center. It is important that a graphic communicator be aware of this tendency, which is especially strong in Western cultures. The optical center may not constitute a dramatically attractive location, but it offers a graphic communicator a generally strong page position that is effective in attracting the reader's eye and beginning the reader's journey through the layout.

Locating the optical center of a page is simple. Begin by identifying the trim page size and then draw a horizontal line 60 percent up from the bottom of the page. This is the optical center line. If a graphic communicator has selected an appropriate symbol to represent the most important part of the message, it should probably be placed at or very near the optical center. And if that communicator can devise a strong graphic treatment and place the element at this particular page position, the effect is not merely additive, but can be exponential, and can help to strongly impress the intended message on a reader.

A caution should be inserted here. Although directions for locating the optical center are rather precise (60 percent from the bottom of a page), in the long run, most professionals temper placement of layout elements by use of mathematics and a pica pole with their experience and their own eyes. If their eye is satisfied with a placement at or near the optical center, that is usually more reliable than a precise measurement made by pica pole. Beginners may want to stay fairly close to the 60 percent distance until they understand its use.

Margins. Generally there are two types of margin schemes; progressive and functional. Most books rely on progressive, or book, margins. Many other publications adopt other margin schemes to meet their particular needs. If you looked inside the library books you measured for the master page assignment, you would have noticed that most of them had margins of unequal size. In fact, you might conclude that they vary in size in a particular manner. That is, that beginning with the smallest margin, which is usually found closest to its accompanying page, margins get larger in a progressive manner as you move around the page, top or head margin to outside to bottom or foot margin. Progressivity in this context means that the gutter margin is the smallest, top margin a bit larger, the outside margin larger still and the bottom clearly the largest of the four. Note that when you look at facing pages the outside margin on the left-hand page is on the left while the outside margin on the right-hand page is on the right. Gutter margins are important when it comes to bookbinding because this is where the book's pages are bound together. Although the gutter margin is the smallest on each page, there are two of them next to one another, and they combine to create a fairly large white space that tends to physically separate the two facing pages. This wide and empty space is not much of a problem in book design (although in paperback books the space is not so wide), but is of more concern in magazine design, where a major problem is that of bridging the gutter to encourage movement of a reader's eye from one page to the next. You may also notice that observing progressive margins may force the middle of the type page a bit higher because the bottom margin is larger than the others and the whole type page seems to slide upwards. The result is a classic book page appearance, with progressive margins and the midpoint of the body of type a little bit higher on the page. This little bit of upward push causes the entire page to relate a bit more strongly to the optical center.

The only way to become proficient in placing margins and using the optical center is to practice. Because books are rather straightforward in their use of space, and because the number and variety of elements on their title pages are likely to be limited, book title pages provide a good practice field for this assignment. Taken together, they require you to locate and use the optical center of a page in an increasingly sophisticated manner.

ASSIGNMENT   *Placing Your Name at the Optical Center of a Page.* The first part of this assignment asks you to place a single line on a book-sized type page. Imagine that the book is your autobiography and the line is simply your name set in type. You have already determined the size of your autobiography by actually measuring the dimensions of similar works, and you have decided which size and shape is best for the tale you have to tell. You have probably learned that books come in all sizes, but that there is a commonality of size within broad categories. Next time you are in a library, take a look at the art books. What do you find? Why are many of them housed on oversized shelves? How about the sizes of paperback books? A stroll through the stacks, browsing and reference rooms, and periodicals area of a library may cause you to conclude that books (as well as newspapers, letterheads, brochures, posters, and most other printed materials) have been around a good long time and that many of the decisions about their basic sizes and shapes have already been made. You may safely conclude that there is some rhyme and reason to selecting appropriate sizes for particular purposes just by looking at the books in a row on the shelves. You don't have to reinvent the wheel each time you plan a project. In fact, that can be dangerous if you make a bad choice. So, although you were free to select the size of the book page for this assignment, it might have been foolish of you to select unusual dimensions unless your decision was based on solid reasoning.

The name of the page on which you are asked to place your name is, for this assignment, what is called the *half-title page.* This was at one time an important page in a book because it helped perform an identity function and established the typography of a work. Finally, although its importance has diminished in recent years, at one time books were often sold without covers to hold down costs to readers. To protect the title page, which tended to appear on the third leaf of a book, a half-title page, the content of which was simply the book's title set in small type, appeared on page 1. In this way, the half-title page became almost a flimsy sort of cover that protected the title page during handling. Few books are now sold this way and so there is little practical use for the page. However, a half-title page still tends to appear in most books because of tradition. Working with such a page offers an opportunity to practice finding an optical center and placing a typographic element on it.

So, apply your knowledge of what others have done for hundreds of years and supplement it with your intelligence in analyzing your own particular needs for your autobiography. Choose the size and shape, sometimes called the *format,* of your autobiography, then decide on margin sizes and assign them, using the appropriate dialogue box of your composition program or by drawing them in on paper if you do not feel comfortable using the computer. When you are finished, you will have created both a type page and a trim page. The area inside the margins, where the content of the page will be placed, is the *type page*, or *live area*. Taken together, the type page and the margins form the *trim page*. The trim page is so named because after all pages are printed and assembled, the sheets on which they are printed will be folded and then trimmed to this size. The margins are not off limits for printed matter, although it pays to remember that most people expect them to be free of type or art. When material appears in them, it is unusual and readers will attach some significance to it. Graphic communicators commonly break into margins with bleed photographs or art to give the material greater magnitude or "punch." Textbook publishers might place visual copy in margins, or create an extra-wide margin on each page for note taking.

Now complete the assignment. Line off your entire page and locate its optical center, about 60 percent up from the bottom of the page. If you are using a computer, you might want to drag a ruler line to this position to provide a visible (but nonprinting) optical center line on the screen. If you are doing paste-up, use a nonreproducing blue pencil to draw the line.

Typeset your name in a word-processing or composition program or trace it from a sample book of type. You will find that you have to make a number of decisions about how you present your name in type. Remember that the impression the type makes on a member or your audience will, to some extent, be the visible you for that person. If the type you select is heavy and dark, perhaps that person will imagine you to be serious; if it is light and airy, the opposite impression might be left. How would you like others to react to you? What race of type will best represent you? A serious Roman or a frivolous novelty typeface? What family? What size? Capitals and lower case or all caps? Italics? Fullface, light, or boldface? Try to select an attractive or interesting family, branch, and size that you feel projects who you are.

When you have discovered the real you, place your name on the optical center line. If you are drawing this assignment, trace your name in a suitable typeface, using one of the many type sample resources available, on the optical center line. When you have finished, assess the result. Move your name if your eye tells you it is not placed correctly.

If you print out your solution on a high-quality printer such as a laser printer, it will be fairly close in appearance to how the page will appear when it is typeset and printed. It is, in fact, the equivalent of a rough layout; in some cases it may be used as a comprehensive if it is good enough to pass muster. Producing one of these copies can help greatly in proofreading. Read it for errors, correct them, and print the revision, if necessary. Don't let an error get past this point or you will likely be unhappy when you do have to make the correction. The farther along in the process you get, the more expensive in time and money it is to go back and repeat the operations necessary to make corrections. And if an error makes it into print and is distributed by the thousands, the humiliation might mean even more to you than money.

Marking Up Type. If you intend to have the material typeset by someone else, you will want to complete marking up the version you created. *Marking up* means giving instruction to the person who will set the type. Remember that you also will have completed a type policy, so that person could, with diligence, work with your stated policy and determine your wishes. But that might take the typesetter a good deal of time, and marking up each portion of your work will save that time and help assure that your instructions are followed.

Marking up consists of identifying the typeface and size and other information that typesetters will need to convert rough copy into typeset characters. Such information includes:

- Type family (Bodoni, English Times, Avant Garde, and so on)

- Family branch (posture, degree of boldness, extension)

- Size (in points)

- Leading (in points)

- Width of lines (this relates to type size and leading, and is usually expressed in picas)

- Indention of paragraphs (usually identified in ems or points)

- Appointment of space (whether column edges are parallel [justified], flush left, and ragged right, centered, and so on)

- Character composition (use of caps and lower case).

Remember to place this information prominently, but outside of the trim page area of your book page. Many professionals put such instructions on an overlay sheet that provides both space for instructions and protection for the work beneath.

Place trim marks on the sheet where they belong, either by using your pica pole and straight edge or by activating the appropriate feature in a composition program. Printers will use these marks to trim the sheet on which the job is printed to the proper size. Hand in the marked-up original of the half-title page. All examples at the end of this section include trim marks.

Dealing with Two-Line and Three-Line Titles. In the second part of this assignment, you will have two-line and three-line titles to deal with, rather than a single line. Although using the optical center appropriately is a bit more difficult when you have more than a single line of type to place on it, you can still produce an effective page by applying a little logic to the problem. When you have more than one line of type, you probably will want to arrange the lines around the optical center so they do not appear to be too high or too low on the page. You almost intuitively know you will be successful if you arrange a two-line message with each line equidistant above or below the optical center line. For a three-line effort it makes sense to place the middle line right on the optical center line and the top line and bottom lines equidistant above and below the middle line. Certainly logic calls for this. If you proceed in this manner and are unhappy with the result, keep adjusting until your eye is happy.

The graphic communicator often has to decide how many lines to allot to titles or headlines. Considerations include both the content of the message and the graphic weight of the headline or title. Practically speaking, it would be rare for any title or headline to require more than three or four lines, and certainly never more than five lines (never say never in typography). A graphic communicator should become adept at dealing with, for example, a long line of type that doesn't fit comfortably on a single line of the page. In such instances, a line break is probably called for. Remember that a comfortable line length, all other things being equal, falls somewhere between two-thirds and three-fourths of the width of the trim page. If a single line is too long, try a smaller size or a more condensed version of the same typeface, or try negative letter spacing. You might be able to edit or rewrite the title. However, after you have visualized the page with the title on it and have selected an appropriate type size for the message, you have made a serious typographic commitment, and you should not make changes willy-nilly simply for expediency. When they are necessary, changes should be given the same thoughtful consideration as the original decision.

Deciding whether a line should be broken into two is a question of meaning as well as appearance. For example, a standing rule of newspaper headline writing is not to end the first line of a two-line headline with a preposition. So, always read the lines to see if they make sense. Finally, line-break decisions require that you become aware of the shapes created by lines of varying length. For example, you should not settle for a top-heavy shape that balances a long line above a very short one. Nor would a very short line atop a very long one be a good solution. They are not very attractive, and they confuse potential readers.

This part of the assignment will give you practice using the optical center when there are multiple lines of type. You are asked to break the book title below into two lines, and then into three lines. When you have solutions you feel are reasonable, try them out by placing them on a page. Use a composition program or trace the lines and paste up your solutions. Remember that the titles should look and read in a natural manner and that they should relate to the optical center of the page. If you measure precisely and place the title on the optical center only to find it doesn't look good to you, go with what your eye tells you. (This is usually good advice in graphics.)

The book's title is:

The First Amendment and the Fourth Estate

When you have solved the two problems, hand in the results.

Dealing with Multiple Page Elements. The third part of the assignment requires additional thought about the use of the optical center when you have more than a single element such as a title, on a page. Other elements might include title, subtitle, author's name, and maybe the publisher's name, address, and logo. Now the question is not only whether or where to break the lines, but how the three or four distinct elements can be accommodated and arranged around the optical center. They must, in the viewer's mind, relate to one another, but at the same time, they can't just be evenly spaced down the page in the same family branch of typeface in the same size. That would be very boring and would not exhibit much in the way of design savvy. At the very least, a graphic communicator would want to use different sizes and a variety of family branches to differentiate elements on a single page. Certainly the most important element, the title, should be placed in close relationship to the optical center. But what about the subtitle and the author's name? And what if the author is as famed as Stephen King? In such cases shouldn't the author's name be prominently featured, with title and subtitle assuming secondary roles?

The matter of grouping arises whenever more than a single element is to be placed on a page. Grouping suggests that elements belonging together conceptually or intellectually should be grouped in space and separated from other, dissimilar elements on the page. A reader should not have to solve a puzzle to learn such things. In practical terms, this means that the amount of space between the several page elements should be clearly greater than the amount of space between parts of the same element. To put it another way, if a two-line title is decided upon, and a one-line subtitle is written to accompany it, there should be less space between the two lines of the title than is placed between the title and subtitle. That way, the user of the page sees two distinct elements and can easily determine their relationship. This assignment requires you to not only use the optical center of the page to enhance the most important element of your book's title page, but to begin thinking about arranging other elements on a page to clearly establish for the reader a hierarchy of page elements which, in turn, suggests a pacing for the reader as he or she moves along the array of elements. To practice, work with the following elements:

The title of a law of mass communication textbook is:

The First Amendment and the Fourth Estate

The subtitle is:

The Law of Mass Media

The authors are:

T. Barron Carter

Marc A. Franklin

Jay B. Wright

Try your hand at arranging these elements on a page so the page is both functional (does its job) and attractive (people respond positively to it by accepting your invitation to read it). Use the page size you selected for your autobiography. Print out the results, complete the mark-up, and hand in an original and a copy. Be prepared to discuss with others the reasons for your decisions.

ASSIGNMENT AIDS   On the following pages, you will find several examples illustrating how you might go about using the optical center for a variety of types of content, from a single line of type to multiple page elements.

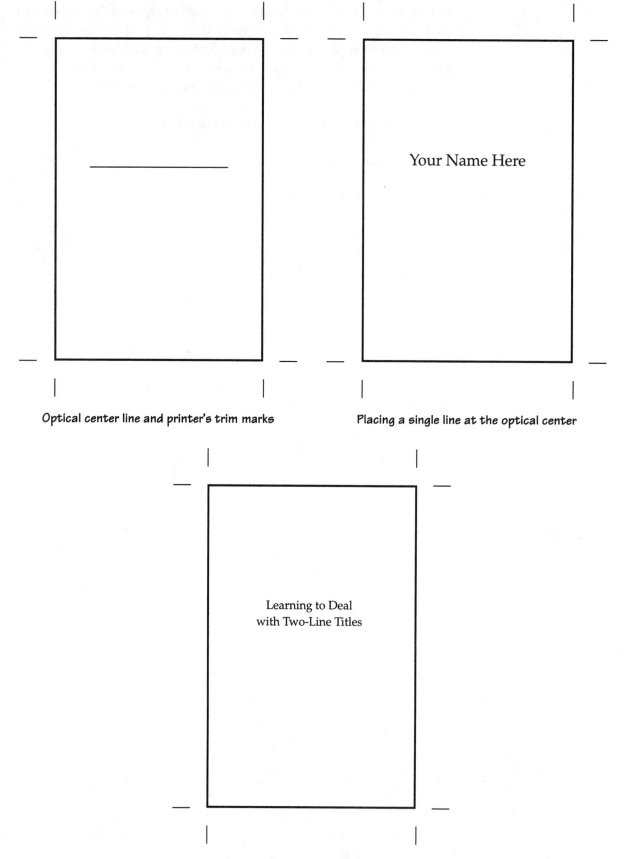

Optical center line and printer's trim marks

Placing a single line at the optical center

Dividing and placing two-line titles

Three-Line Titles
Should Make Sense
and Be Attractive

Learning to Deal
with Multiple Elements

———————

Your Name Here

Publisher's Name
City and Nation

Dividing multiple-line titles

Placing multiple elements on a page

6 AUTOBIOGRAPHY TITLE PAGE

OBJECTIVES Thinking about layout space and how type (and art) can be placed within it to both transfer meaning effectively and be attractive is important work for the graphic communicator. Crafting a title page for your autobiography will allow you to apply some of the techniques professional designers use and to generalize some of the skills you learned in previous assignments. Because this assignment will bring you closer to completing the autobiography package, it can provide you an opportunity to see the consequences of some of the choices you made and expressed in your type policy.

TO HAND IN Hand in a title page rough for your autobiography, including type mark-up and trim marks.

ASSIGNMENT You presumably have worked up a bunch of thumbnails that exhibit an evolution of your plan for some of the pages of your autobiography. A page shape has emerged in the form of a trim page and a type page. You have worked on your page margin scheme and probably settled on traditional progressive book margins. The physical outline of your autobiography has thus been set, albeit loosely. You can still make changes if they are warranted, but what you have to this point resulted from thoughtful consideration of the problem, and you don't want to alter it without a pretty fair reason. You can put your earlier reasoning to the test by working on the title page and seeing how your typography and visual materials (if any) will work in that space. If they seem to work, you can begin to work in earnest on your finished layout. If not, it's back to the drawing board to make revisions.

You have a working title for your autobiography, which you submitted earlier, and a tentative choice for a subtitle. Of course you know the name of the author of your autobiography. You don't know who will bid high enough to win the honor of publishing it, but you can now assume that it will be Journalism Press, with offices in Paris, London, and Beijing.

This assignment requires you to design a title page for your autobiography. Begin by thinking first and then capturing your best thoughts on thumbnail sketches. When you have good solutions on thumbnails, you can then begin to work in a composition program, if you like, or use paste-up techniques to create and then assemble page elements in full size. Remember that only a few elements commonly appear on the title pages of books, and that there can (and should) be ample white space around them.

There is one final consideration. Perhaps you ran across some facing page titles (a two-page spread) in some of the works you examined in the library. Or perhaps you found visual copy on some title pages. Those are options that might appeal to you, although most title pages are single pages (especially when they have only text). If visual copy is dictated, a two-page spread might be required to achieve optimum effectiveness. However, visual copy is not often dictated for autobiographical works, but is saved for more highly dramatic works (*Cosmos* by Carl Sagan comes to mind, with the need to hint at the billions of worlds capable of sustaining life that are possible in the universe). If you have dramatic visual content, you probably can't afford to ignore it. But probably your best choice, at this stage in your career, is to go with a single page. If you decide on visual copy within that single page, it should probably be subordinated to the title or consigned to background duty.

You can profitably begin your work by deciding which of the elements on the title page is the most important. That element is a good choice for placement at or near the optical center. As you begin to place other elements on the page, keep in mind the goal of establishing a pleasing relationship between and among page elements. Consider the following advice as you are thinking about the appearance of your title page.

- Group similar elements so they will be perceived as belonging together and separate distinct elements on each page. For example, the title and subtitle should be closer to one another than both of them should be to the author's name.

- Use contrast to both attract the viewer's eye and move it along. You might accomplish this by giving additional size, boldness, or color to the more important elements.

- Align edges of elements either by arraying them around a center line drawn vertically through the middle of the layout or aligning them flush on a margin. At this point, you might want to use centering as your alignment scheme; it's not always as exciting as other arrangements might be, but it is usually safe.

- Use repetition as means of effectively presenting your composition as a unified whole. The easiest way to accomplish this is to restrict the number of different typefaces you use on the title page, or perhaps use only one.

Now is also the time to assess your selection of typefaces and sizes. It is important to not lose sight of the fact the type will be seen on a page that is about 6 by 9 inches, held at arm's length. Type may not have to be as large as 72 to 96 points to be effective in such a frame. In fact, you might want to begin your thinking at about 36 points for the most important title page element. Other less important elements can be smaller in size, or otherwise toned down.

Even though margins are not much of a consideration on pages where there is no text, put them in anyway, because they will indicate when a line of type is becoming too long for comfort or when the elements of a page are getting too high or too low in the space. For starters, restrict line lengths to about two-thirds to three-quarters of the width of the page, even though doing so might require you to break your title into two lines, which in turn might require you to adjust the placement of other elements to maintain pleasing relationships and appearances.

It might be helpful to begin your thinking about this assignment by closing your eyes and imagining how you wish the page to appear. When you have that mental image, move along to the thumbnail sketch stage. Rely on thumbnails to help you make your graphic decisions and then use them to guide you in the production phase. Only when you have a firm idea for a solid page should you begin working at the computer, if you decide to produce your title page in that manner, or at the layout table, if you choose to use traditional page assembly methods. The key is to give yourself plenty of time for thoughtful contemplation of all possibilities before committing yourself to a solution. This advice holds especially true when you are working at a computer, where it is easy to become trapped in a virtually endless cycle of moving elements and printing the results.

When you have completed your work and have produced a suitable rough, hand it in along with the thumbnails that guided you. Make certain that everyone who sees your work can understand what you are trying to do by adding trim marks and type mark-up instructions. Placing trim marks shows the trim page, or final size of the work, and helps the printer to print, fold, bind, and trim the work. These marks can be placed on your work by hand or automatically by a number of composition programs (in which case they will show up on the laser printer sheet only if your page size is smaller than the paper on which your title is printed). Some programs will insert trim marks and register marks, as well as a tonal scale that will help the printer print the work to your specifications. Complete marking up the title page by identifying the typefaces and type sizes you are using. Do all mark-up neatly and legibly, outside the trim marks. (If there is no room on the sheet, use a separate sheet or an overlay.)

ASSIGNMENT AIDS   On the following pages, you will find several examples illustrating the effects of grouping similar elements.

Title of Book

Subtitle of Book

Author's Name

Publisher's Name

City or Nation

Title page exhibiting no contrast of size and no evidence of grouping of elements

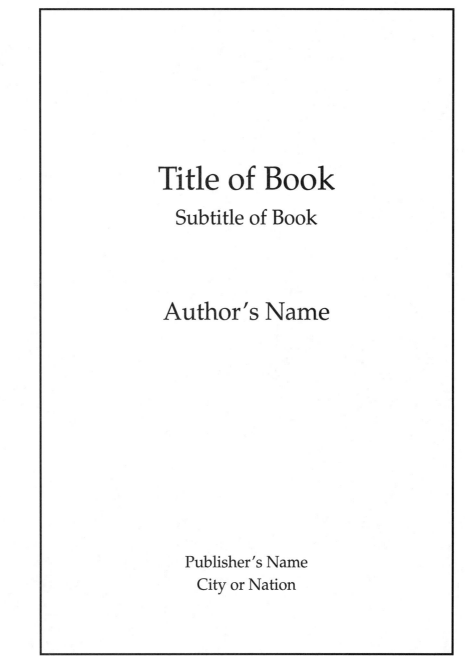

Title of Book
Subtitle of Book

Author's Name

Publisher's Name
City or Nation

Title page exhibiting contrast of size and evidence of grouping of elements

7 PROCESSING PHOTOGRAPHS

OBJECTIVES
This assignment will help you learn to determine the amount of space that visual copy will take up in a layout before the fully processed visual copy is actually available to you. Learning how to scale a photograph will enable you to make visual copy assignments (photographs, illustrations, and so on) so that when they are prepared and submitted, they can be slipped right into layout spaces you have allocated to them. Your ability to allocate layout space accurately, prior to beginning production, will result in much greater satisfaction and much less stress and dislocation for everyone involved.

TO HAND IN
You will solve and hand in your solution to the problem at the end of this assignment. You must show all work to receive full credit.

ASSIGNMENT BACKGROUND
Much visual copy regularly seen in consumer publications consists of photographs, although graphs, tables, charts, drawings, and maps (collectively called *infographics*) appear commonly. Most photographs in magazines such as *Time*, *Newsweek*, *National Geographic*, *Sports Illustrated*, and so on are sharp, clear, colorful, and excellent accompaniments to the text. The best of them transfer ideas embedded in the image across to you effectively and efficiently. In fact, although their storytelling ability may not even rise to the level of consciousness in the average reader's mind, this can make them even more powerful in transferring meaning. It should not surprise you to learn that good photographs are not easy to come by. The best photographers and artists have devoted careers to perfecting the skill of consistently producing high-quality photographs. Their work is in demand and costly, but it is often worth the expense because of the effect it can have on reception of an idea by an audience. Learning how to make such determinations is a crucial skill for a graphic communicator to develop.

The definition of a good photograph depends to a great extent on the context in which it will appear. For example, a badly blurred and out-of-focus picture of a young girl and boy falling to their deaths as a fire escape gave way beneath them was a dramatic addition to the news of the day a number of years ago. But an out-of-focus picture would be sadly out of place in an *Architectural Digest* spread featuring the home of a well-known Hollywood celebrity. A newspaper or news magazine editor would jump at the opportunity to run the former, while the editor of a nonnews magazine might not give the latter a second look. Graphic communicators must be prepared to assess photographs in the appropriate context and apply quality judgments if they intend to use visuals effectively. This skill cannot be taught, but must be learned.

Fortunately, there are some qualities of good photographs that usually can be identified. If they are missing, it is unlikely that the photograph will be suitable for publication and the graphic communicator risks little by discarding it. If the qualities are there, the communicator can be much more confident using the photograph. These qualities can be defined along two dimensions:

- Content considerations

- Technical considerations

Content. Content qualities define the journalistic or storytelling capability of the photograph and include such matters as composition, lighting, dramatic impact, as well as the more subtle cues the viewer needs to interpret the content. For example, perspective hints at depth in the photograph, which in turn helps create reality. Sometimes a photographer wants to get rid of an intrusive background and manipulates the depth of field to blur the background, deemphasizing it.

Technical. Technical qualities are related directly to whether the photograph is capable of being reproduced well. Such qualities include proper density, a wide contrast range, sharpness, and true-to-reality color. The Buddhist commitment to the middle way is not an inappropriate metaphor in this context. Technical qualities should cluster around an ideal. For example, negatives that were exposed properly are more likely to produce suitable photographic images than will overexposed or underexposed negatives. A contrast range that provides for detail in both shadows and highlights is also desired. Sharpness is essential, although graininess can be used to good effect in appropriate applications. And, finally, colors that are realistic and true-to-life as well as true to the expectations of the audience are apt to communicate better than those that aren't.

A few rules of thumb for selecting photographs, or other visual materials, might include the following:

- If the technical quality is not exemplary, don't use it.

- If it is acceptable in technical quality, and you must use it, run it a column narrower than you had planned, thus deemphasizing it.

- If it is technically exemplary and its content is outstanding and powerful, run it a column wider than you had planned, thus emphasizing it.

- If its content is outstanding or powerful, that is usually more important than technical considerations, especially in news situations or where the depiction of drama is needed.

- If the content of the visual copy is central to the story and significantly enhances it, it runs. The more peripheral it is to the story, the less necessary it is.

There is nothing quite so useless as a trite photograph, because it communicates so little. Unfortunately, such photographs appear too often, given scanners, digital cameras, desktop publishing programs, and amateur graphic communicators. Examples of these are seen daily. The only person who can save an unsuspecting audience from having to waste time dealing with inferior visuals is the graphic communicator/editor. He or she must never lose sight of the goal of producing strong, simple, concise, and innovative graphic packages that smoothly integrate art and text and help the audience understand what a client is spending a good deal of money to say. A piece of art that complements well-written and well-presented copy is a key to making the package worthwhile.

Cropping and Sizing. It is a rare photograph that will not benefit from thoughtful cropping. Rare also are photographs that come to the graphic communicator for use in precisely the right size or shape for the layout they will anchor. Cropping and sizing are processes that help graphic communicators become certain the visual copy says what is intended and that it fits in the appropriate place in a layout. *Cropping* is the process of editing for content, and *sizing* is the process of getting the photograph to fit in a layout. Cropping is an editorial operation, although it includes making sure that the service provider receives clear instructions so the cropped photograph can be reproduced as the graphic communicator has envisioned it. Judicious cropping can eliminate unwanted parts of a photograph, because they contain inappropriate content or technical errors that can't be dealt with by other means. Of course, by eliminating one portion of a photo, the graphic communicator has, in the process, emphasized what remains.

Sizing of the photograph is closely tied to proper reproduction and so is more closely tied to the printing operation than to the editorial. It is attended to only after cropping. Sizing tells the graphic communicator how much layout space has to be reserved for the photograph to fit. For example, you might have before you a photograph that is 8 × 10, but you want to use it in a layout space that is only 4 inches wide. You want to use the entire 8 × 10 content and don't want to crop the photograph to precisely 4 × 5 (that would require cropping away 75 percent of it). In this case, it is simple to see that if you reduce the entire photograph to 50 percent of it original, size, it will fit. In this instance, 50 percent of 8 is 4, and 50 percent of 10 is 5, or 4 × 5. To accomplish this mental feat, you relied on your understanding of the simple principle of proportion, which states that when you photographically reduce or enlarge a four-sided space, the lengths of the sides may change, but they remain in identical proportion to one another. So, if you have a rectangle that is 4 inches by 6 inches, and you enlarge it to two times, which is 200 percent of its original size, the 4-inch side becomes 8 inches and the 6-inch side becomes 12 inches. The enlarged size is 8 × 12. The proportion of the length to the width remained the same. There is a simple equation that helps in calculating this.

$$\frac{\text{original width}}{\text{original depth}} = \frac{\text{desired/reproduction width}}{\text{desired/reproduction depth}}$$

Assume that for the preceding problem, we have an 8 × 10 photograph, all of which we would like to use in a layout, and we know that we have only 4 inches of width in the layout available for it. (In the case of most newspapers, this would be about the width of two columns, a very common width.) How deep a space must be allowed for the photograph to fit? If we plug in the numbers, we get:

$$\frac{8}{10} = \frac{4}{x} \qquad \begin{aligned} 8x &= 40 \\ x &= 5 \end{aligned}$$

Thus, the space that must be set aside in the layout is 4 inches wide and 5 inches deep. The graphic communicator, knowing only the size of the photograph and the width of the space in the layout where it must go, can do this simple problem and leave enough space. The same formula can be used to determine how much width must be allowed for the depth of a photograph if the layout space cannot be altered along that dimension.

The final step in the process is to calculate the percentage of enlargement or reduction that will have to take place if the photograph is to fit properly. Completing this step helps the prepress person or service provider to set the copy camera/process camera or scanner correctly so the proper size film can be made. Getting this step right can save a good deal of grief later on. It serves as a guide and is also a double check. Because the copy camera or scanner has to be set precisely to produce a given enlargement or reduction, the calculation can be phrased as a focus (F) that informs the back-shop camera or scanner operator where to focus. The formula is a simple one:

$$F(ocus) = \frac{\text{desired width}}{\text{original width}} \qquad F = 4/8$$
$$F = 50$$

This information, $F = 50$, is translated by the person who will make the film the proper size.

Because all of this information is crucial, it should be placed prominently on a mark-up sheet. An overlay sheet, which protects the print, is often used as a mark-up sheet, and if it is mounted on a stiff backing the photograph will be doubly protected. Alternatively, you could put the information on a separate sheet and attach it to the back of the photograph. It is important that you never write with a pencil or pen on the back of the photograph, as this might deform the emulsion enough to be visible when the art is reproduced. The same happens when you use a paperclip on a photograph. Never use staples, either.

Marking up visual copy allows the service provider to identify the visual copy properly, change it (crop and size) as needed, apply the proper screens and so on, and be certain the film is placed in the right spot in the layout and printed as the graphic communicator wishes. Such mark-up is analogous to what you would do with a manuscript you want to be typeset. To do a good job, the mark-up should address such matters as:

- A slugline or identifying name
- The original size of the photograph, with crop marks in plain sight
- The desired or reproduction size of the photograph, indicated by the crop marks
- The screen size and screen type that are to be used
- Special finishes (silhouette or outline, vignette, special geometric shape, and so on)
- The page and page position it will occupy in a publication
- The amount of enlargement or reduction that is required

ASSIGNMENT Try your skill at sizing by solving the following problem.

You have sent a photographer out on assignment and she has returned with a beautiful 10×8 waterfront scene. It needs cropping, however. So, you crop $3\frac{1}{2}$ inches from the width and $2\frac{1}{2}$ inches from the depth. Now it is perfect from the standpoint of content. You plan to run it across a full magazine page, 8 inches, as a three-margin bleed. How deep a space must you allow in the layout? Assume the photograph will be the only visual copy that will appear on page 18 of a publication. Also assume you will use a 120-line round-dot screen. Include in the mark-up the percentage of enlargement or reduction that will be required. Hand in your solution on a separate sheet, showing all of your work.

8 AUTHOR'S BLURB AND PHOTOGRAPH AND CHAPTER OPENING PAGES

OBJECTIVES This assignment will give you the opportunity to try out your newly developed skills of cropping, scaling, and marking up photographs. You will practice writing briefly about yourself and you will produce a completed, ready for filming and printing, chapter of your autobiography, complete with chapter opening page.

As soon as you have completed one part of this assignment, you will have portions of a complete work in all stages of production, from finished to not even begun. Keeping track of them all will give you practice in managing a job from beginning to end and at all points in between. Merely keeping track of all parts of the complete assignment may challenge you. Perhaps you can think of a written means of keeping track of your progress on this assignment. The decisions you have made to this point are the type you will make as a professional. You know that some of them have been good ones, and others may have turned out worse than you might have wished. You now know that if you aren't satisfied with what you have accomplished and believe that you can do better, you can go back to the beginning and work your way forward. This process is always a challenge for professionals. The lesson is that if you spend sufficient time thinking before beginning production you may actually save time in the long run. The decisions you have made that turned out well for you should help build confidence in your abilities.

TO HAND IN Hand in the back inside panel of the book jacket (photograph and blurb) as well as a finished chapter rough, including the chapter opening page. Everything should be marked up, and it should conform to your type policy.

ASSIGNMENT **Author's Photograph and Blurb.** It is now time for you to complete some of your autobiography project and take on another challenge. The inside back cover of virtually all book jackets contains a picture of the author and a short paragraph about him or her. This short biographical paragraph, which tells you a little bit about the author and his or her credentials, is called a *blurb*. The picture that usually accompanies the blurb gives readers a glimpse of his or her physical features. To complete this assignment you will need a photograph of yourself. It can be in virtually any form if you intend to complete this assignment on a computer, but if you do not intend to use a computer, you should have a print that can be sized and cropped. This part of the assignment asks you to crop and size your image properly and pass that information along to the production people. If your image is stored in a folder in the computer, use Adobe Photoshop or another similar program to crop and size it and complete any other alterations you feel necessary. Then you can import it into your composition program for proper placement on the inside back panel of your book jacket. If you are working with paste-ups, size your selected photo and use a piece of gray construction paper to represent it in your layout.

Completing this panel of your book jacket should not pose much of a problem. Be certain that you have checked in the library to get an idea of the normal width of such a panel. Its depth will be the depth of your book. Any size photograph that fits will do, but be sure to leave enough room on the panel to hold the blurb. When you see what others have offered as a blurb for themselves, get busy and write one for yourself. Then go back the panel to complete your work. Place your photograph and blurb as you wish, but remember what countless others have done. You are not bound to imitate them, but if you decide to strike out in a new way, you should probably be prepared to defend your choices. You must follow your type policy for this important part of your work. If the book jacket copy is not included in your type policy, you will want to add it. Whether you set your name in display type under or over your photograph or whether you don't is not of great concern. Study possibilities by making up thumbnails before you begin. Hand in your results, marked up properly.

Chapter Opening Pages. As you go about producing finished versions of the chapter opener and the remaining pages of the chapter, you will want to turn back to your master pages, or to the templates you created for these pages for an earlier assignment. Recheck them to assure that they are as you intended and that they address such matters as trim page size, type page size, headers, and footers as well as page numbers. As you examine how others have presented the initial page of a chapter, you may note that most of them have a very large upper margin and begin the page copy a substantial distance from the top of the trim page. Also, most of them place a chapter number in the blank space at the top and some include a chapter title.

As with the book jacket portion of this assignment, be sure you have followed your type policy. If you paste up your work, you will want to print out a typeset-like version of your copy in a word processing program, assigning family characteristics, branches, width of line, initial letters, and so on. Print it out and use the printout to complete pasting up. Mark up the result, preferably using an overlay. If you choose to work in a composition program, you will want to make all necessary preparations of the page and then complete mark-up, again on an overlay.

Hand in the blurb panel, chapter opening page, and the remainder of the chapter. In addition, because you are nearing the end of this project, you can begin making certain that the rest of your autobiography copy is clean and ready for printing (copyedited and proofread) and that everything is in order.

ASSIGNMENT AIDS   On page 60, you will find an example of a chapter opening page and an author's blurb and photograph represented on a book jacket overlay.

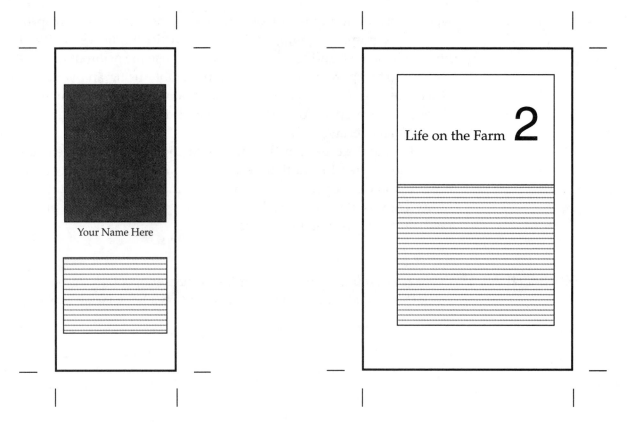

Your Name Here

Author's photo/blurb

Life on the Farm **2**

Chapter opening page

9 PREPARING THUMBNAILS OF BOOK JACKET AND SPINE OF AUTOBIOGRAPHY

OBJECTIVE The objective of this assignment is for you to visualize a book jacket and spine for your autobiography by bringing together and organizing appropriate examples of art and typography to create an attractive sales tool that represents the content of your autobiography and also says something about you.

TO HAND IN Prepare and hand in at least five thumbnails of a book jacket and spine. The instructor will comment on them, and, after consultation, you will select one to make into a rough. Although a full-sized version is not assigned now, the next assignment will ask you to create a rough.

ASSIGNMENT BACKGROUND It is not true that we don't judge a book by its cover. We do it all the time, especially in the popular paperback book publishing field, and we have done so since books first appeared. Although simple leather covers, perhaps with a geometric design, were once a standard of beauty and attractiveness, many older science fiction readers will recall colorful, and sometimes lurid, paperback book covers with scenes of horror portrayed on them. Usually it was an alien from off-planet either tearing apart an Army regiment with its bare hands or a warty monster carting off a beautiful, screaming woman. Gothic romances, readers know, often feature handsome men with muscles bulging, standing over or holding beautiful, swooning, women dressed in revealing gowns, and whose hair softly cascades here and there, while the river meanders gently along the plantation grounds in the background, and fire shoots from every window in the place. . . .

Although hard-bound book covers tend to be pretty plain, a good number of them are encased in colorful book jackets before they appear on bookstore shelves. The book jackets are often protected by a plastic film. Publishers take the time to develop and print such covers because it has long been known that packaging can attract consumers and influence their buying decisions. In fact, settling on the appropriate presentation of a book jacket can be a very important decision. The cover of a book (or a periodical, for that matter) is the first, and often the only, chance a graphic communicator has to attract potential buyers and get them to take a look. While at one time it was prohibitively expensive to print attractive book covers cheaply, the inclusion of full-color photographs and illustrations is now both possible and relatively inexpensive, thanks to advances in printing and other technologies. The generally increased competition for peoples' attention and dollars has led to the development of book jackets as both promotional billboards and protective packaging for the printed work.

Remember that the main purpose of a book jacket is to catch the reader's eye as the vital first step in getting him or her to commit time and money to obtaining the offering. Of course, as with most such matters in the graphic arts, if everyone sets his or her covers to shouting out with bold type, vivid color, and exciting or unusual art, the boldness and extravagance across the bookstore tends to blend together and can overwhelm any single offering. The customer's eye then may see only a jumble of art, type, and color and have difficulty focusing on any particular work.

Applying a standard and timeworn piece of advice works well here. That is the K-I-S-S standard, which stands for keep it simple, stupid. Applying K-I-S-S, while keeping in mind your target audience as well as your wish to create a cover that reflects the high quality of autobiographical work your talent has produced, will result in a successful effort on this assignment. Of course, you have little more to work with than a bit of visual copy and a few words to accomplish your goal of showcasing the content in a way that will attract a potential reader. So choose carefully.

ASSIGNMENT   Your assignment is to design a book jacket for your autobiography, including a spine. Because you want your package to be the equal of any other, to attract attention and touch off a buying frenzy, you probably could benefit from a trip to a campus bookstore, or to a library's browsing room, or even to a nearby Barnes & Noble or Waldenbooks to see what constitutes modern book and paperback cover design. Get a feel for the competition in the market as well as what appeals to you. Then apply some creativity and begin preliminary work on the book jacket for your autobiography. Your specific assignment is to submit five thumbnails for comment. The jacket will, for purposes of this assignment, include the front cover and spine only, and not the back cover, which is often a full-dress or full face portrait of the author or is covered with reasons why one should buy the book, perhaps because it received "two thumbs up."

You are free to use virtually any visual copy you find or create for yourself. Because you are not an artist, you do not have to produce a professional-quality piece of art. If you have access to a scanner or a

Web resource, you may use art you are able to find in those places. Of course, if you were a professional you would not be able to take the work of others without recognizing their efforts, either by giving them credit or by paying them for the right to use their work. Using the intellectual creations of others is a matter for the law of copyright.

Although there has been little published research on book covers and their attractive power in the market, it is pretty well established that when it comes to magazines on newsstand racks, the average person makes a buying decision in only a few seconds, based largely on the cover. Other research on magazine covers tells us that faces on the cover, especially beautiful, handsome, or striking ones, sell magazines, and that almost as helpful is visual copy that crystallizes an idea for the average browser. You may assume that these findings can be generalized to book jackets.

Although this is not part of this assignment, be thinking ahead to submitting your entire autobiography package, which will complete this project. Keep track of all of your design plans, policies, copy, and so on so that you can easily revise and print parts of your package along with all appropriate supplementary material.

ASSIGNMENT AID   Here is an example of a book cover and spine.

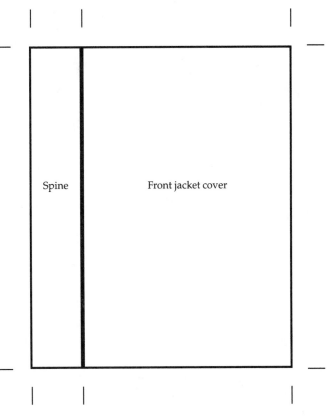

Spine

Front jacket cover

Book jacket cover and spine

10 BOOK JACKET COVER AND SPINE

OBJECTIVE   In this assignment you will convert a thumbnail into a rough. You are also asked to finalize your type policy and make certain that all elements in your work are addressed by the type policy and that all type policies are followed.

TO HAND IN   Hand in two roughs of your book jacket cover and spine, with art and appropriate typography.

ASSIGNMENT   You recently handed in five thumbnails of your autobiography's book jacket cover and spine. You are now asked to select your two best thumbnail efforts, based on your thinking and the comments offered by the instructor, and create a rough from each of the two. Rely on the decisions you made about your autobiography's type policy, as you have developed it to this point. The roughs are to appear exactly as called for in your thumbnails and must follow the type policy you have developed. There are no exceptions. What you have placed on the thumbnail and where you place elements on the rough must coincide. Of course you may, as an outcome of seeing your choices in a full-sized version, come to believe you have made a horrible mistake (a type that is too large or too small, a piece of copy that obscures a crucial portion of a photograph, and so on). Do not change your work if you find this is true. Complete the roughs. If this happened to you as a professional, you would make changes, perhaps by returning to square one, either on the type policy or on the thumbnail. You will be evaluated solely on how faithfully you bring to life the concepts you worked into your thumbnails and type policy. Now is not the time to become creative. Follow the path you set for yourself. After you've done that you may wish to become reflective, and if you feel the roughs are not what you thought they would be, become critical and move toward something more in keeping with your original thoughts and desires. There is nothing wrong, at this stage, with changing your mind, but don't do it on this assignment without paying attention to the rules outlined in the next paragraph. If you make a change, you must submit both roughs for this assignment. Also submit a final copy of your type policy.

If you are satisfied with your type policy and with one of the roughs of the jacket cover and spine, your assignment is complete. If you are not satisfied with either the appearance of the rough or the type policy, for any reason, go back to the beginning and work your way through. You will by now want to be thinking ahead to submitting the entire autobiography package, which will complete this project. Review your plans and policies and the page elements you have generated.

11 FINAL ASSEMBLY
OF THE AUTOBIOGRAPHY

OBJECTIVE   This assignment will bring your autobiography project to completion. The exercise requires you to be certain that all components are the appropriate size and that they appear in finished form, as you had planned. The completed project will require your layout skills as you produce the book jacket (front, spine, and blurb) and ready it for further processing, such as filming and printing. You will also work with the title page, chapter opening pages, and text pages and follow those pages through to completion.

When you have completed your work, think back over the past several weeks and how you carried the project to this point. Your experiences on this project may alert you to the consequences of making decisions early on that prove to be nonproductive or that cause you an inordinate amount of work to bring to fruition. Reflecting on your experiences now may help you learn how to avoid problems with bad decisions in the future. Decisions you made that turned out well will help you develop confidence in yourself, and that is the hallmark of a professional.

TO HAND IN   Hand in all book jacket materials on a single sheet, sized and folded, and wrapped around a suitably sized book, as a book jacket would be. All inside materials, including title page, chapter opener, and chapter copy should be trimmed and bound (with tape or thread, as you choose) as they might be if they were parts of a real book. The pages should then be slipped into the pages of the suitably sized book as if they were actually pages of the book. The result should give you a pretty fair idea of how your autobiography might appear if it were printed.

ASSIGNMENT   Assemble your rough layouts. Trim them to size, and complete all folds (of the jacket and blurb overleaf), and then assemble all materials in book form (a thin book) as well as you are able. Wrap the cover material around an appropriate book and place the trimmed pages into the book. Imagine that you will be handing this copy to a client for final approval. Make certain that you also submit your type policy and that you have included complete mark-up instructions on a separate sheet or on an overlay.

Be prepared to present your autobiography to the class.

12 PROOFREADING

OBJECTIVE
As a project moves nearer the printing stage, it becomes more and more important that there be no errors in it. Errors that are not corrected before printing begins might well be reproduced thousands of times and sent out to the public. In such cases, every revolution of the press becomes another disaster, and that can darken anyone's day. Such disasters are preventable, but you must learn and carefully practice the skill called *proofreading* if you hope to avoid them. If properly accomplished, proofreading can save you from what might be called a humiliating "death of 1,000 cuts," as you witness imperfect printed materials being distributed under your name, possibly by the thousands. Proofreading is one of the more valuable skills a graphic communicator can develop. Although it is not at all creative or glamorous, doing it conscientiously can mark the difference between a job well done and one done poorly, or even one that is unacceptable and has to be redone. Good proofreading can save you time, money, and professional embarrassment.

TO HAND IN
Correct the galley proof at the end of the discussion and hand in the corrected galley.

ASSIGNMENT
BACKGROUND
Proofreading, or reading proof, is the process of checking text and visual copy for accuracy to prevent errors from being printed and distributed to the public. Careful proofreading is your responsibility. Most printers will not go forward with a job until they receive formal approval from you. That approval comes in the form of your signature on a proof. This places responsibility squarely on you, because when you sign off, you free the printer from liability for at least a good portion of any errors in the copy and from any harm that flows from them.

The need for proofreading arises out of the simple fact that humans are fallible and make mistakes. Unfortunately, even little errors take on great magnitude if they are distributed to the public by the thousands. At the very least, they hint at incompetence. Who can trust you in great matters if you can't spell correctly? Graphic communicators may be no more prone to error than other professionals, but their errors are unusually public in nature.

The demands placed on communication professionals increase the likelihood that they will make mistakes. Many formal studies show that the greater the stress on individuals, the greater the potential for error. Pressures can come from a variety of sources, including the demands of clients, colleagues, and supervisors. Graphic communicators can also burden themselves by setting difficult-to-attain personal and professional goals. (Knowing as much as possible about graphic communication is a good reality check that can help you avoid setting unrealistic goals.) Finally, the nature of printing production—with its tight budgets, deadlines, and need to attend to numerous minute details—adds to the pressure. Errors inevitably creep into printed projects at one stage or another, and so it is obvious that graphic communicators must learn to deal with them calmly and deliberately.

Proofing offers what may be a final opportunity to make certain that your typeset copy is exactly as you wish it to be. Accomplishing that can save your bacon. There is also a parallel proofing system for visual copy. Accurate proofreading of both verbal and visual copy is a necessary skill that must be learned early in your professional career.

Proofreading typeset copy is much like copyediting raw copy. Both editors and printers work to similar ends, which is to assure that the copy will be perfect in every way. But the two processes are not identical. One obvious difference is that they rely on different sets of symbols to make changes. A more fundamental difference is that copyediting is located in the editorial stream, when all is still relatively fluid. Proofreading is located in the production or printing stream, when it is not uncommon to have copy pretty much set in stone. Errors made in the editorial stream can be corrected relatively cheaply and easily, but as a project moves closer to printing, correction costs can mount rapidly simply because you must retrace so many steps. Making corrections in the later stages of production adds nothing to the effectiveness of the job, but subtracts significantly from its efficient completion.

Fortunately (or unfortunately) printers have had hundreds of years of experience with the consequences of poor error-detection procedures, and a number of points have been built into the process where someone is required to examine copy and affirm that it is correct.

Commonly, there are two distinct stages of production in which proofing is done: prepress and on press. Of course you can clearly see that making a correction when the job is on press requires retracing many more steps than making corrections earlier, in the prepress stage.

The names and uses of each kind of proof should be learned at the beginning. The more common prepress proofs are, in the order you are likely to receive them:

- Galley proofs or galleys

- Revises (of the corrected galleys)

- Page proofs and bluelines or dyluxes.

Once the plates are on the press and it is up and running, proofs are called *press proofs*. There are also proofs for art copy and color printing.

Galley proofs, or galleys, are type proofs pulled after the marked-up copy (the typewritten or word-processed copy you generated and sent along for typesetting) has been converted into typeset form. They are the first proofs available from a service provider. Reading galleys requires that you make certain the content of the typeset copy is identical to the typewritten or word-processed copy you submitted to the typesetter, and that all of your mark-up instructions have been observed. Errors that the typesetter made must be called out and appropriate proofing marks must be used to alert the typesetter to make corrections.

Generally, one of two systems of making corrections is used: book or guideline. If the typeset copy is relatively clean, all the proofreader needs to do is make a small mark within a typeset line at the point of the error and then enter the symbol that calls for its correction in one of the margins. If the copy is dirtier, or if there is a possibility that the typesetter might be confused as to which correction is which, guideline proofs dictate that you make a small mark where the error was found and draw a fine line from there out to one of the margins, where the appropriate correction symbol is entered at the end of the line.

When you receive galleys, be aware they have already been proofread in the typesetting house and all errors that the typesetter might have made in setting the type should have been caught and corrected. So galley proofs should be relatively clean. Still, it is your responsibility to read galleys carefully for accuracy. Many printing jobs can be improved in appearance if widows and orphans are removed, and figuring how to accomplish that may be one of your proofreading tasks. But your most significant responsibility is to make certain that the typeset copy is identical to what you initially approved for typesetting and that it is error-free. Of course, if you discover that a passage contains a libel, if crucial information is incorrect, or if there is some other major shortcoming, it must be addressed at whatever point in the process it is found. The expense of a libel suit or the loss of credibility that an egregious error can lead to is good enough reason to make such corrections.

If you have made many proofreading marks and if your galley proofs look fairly dirty or cluttered, you might ask that the errors be corrected and proofs of the corrected galleys be returned to you for a second look. Such proofs are called *revises*, and they might be indicated if accuracy is particularly crucial.

When initial proofing has been completed and corrections have been made (to art as well as typeset copy), type and art will be assembled into pages, based on your layout instructions. Proofs of laid-out pages can be made, or pulled, so you can see that all art and type copy is properly placed, that page numbers, decorative devices, headers and footers, cutlines, and so on are correct and placed as you ordered. By this stage, of course, you have moved beyond correcting to observing relationships between and among elements in the layout, and calling out those bits of art or type that seem out of place. These proofs are often in the form of dylux or blueline proofs, which are pulled after film has been made and negatives stripped in properly. The negatives are placed on top of a proofing paper and strong light is shined through them. The light that comes through the film creates a visible image on the paper. This is an important proof to read carefully. If errors are spotted, circle them in red or in some way that stands out and return the proof for assessment and correcting. This proof may be your last relatively inexpensive opportunity to correct errors.

The final proof is the *press proof*. which is really one of the first good copies of the printed work to roll off the press. As the first copies come off, printers grab them and, based on what they see, adjust inking or registration so that the production stage can begin in earnest. You can arrange with a printer to be on hand for this important event. When the press is inked properly and the paper is feeding well and as the press crew settles in to tend the press for the production run, a printed sheet can easily be taken from the press and brought to you for comment. If serious concerns are raised, you can always stop the press; although if you've applied yourself diligently throughout the process this should not be necessary. Still, it is the last-chance proof, and it is always a good idea to be there for this event. It many even be required if one of your valued clients has arranged with you to supervise a tricky run involving, say, color halftones or multiple printing techniques. Your being on hand for the start of such a run is a no-brainer, especially early in your career. If you are there, you not only can read proofs, but you can learn a good deal about the mysteries of printing. It can be an invigorating change of pace to get out of the office and see how other professionals work on projects you wrote, edited, and designed.

ASSIGNMENT   This assignment asks you to try your hand at reading galley proofs. Assume the copy is exactly as you have written and edited it, that it has been approved by all persons in your agency's or company's chain of command. Assume also that you have given the compositor clean copy, properly marked up. Imagine that the type has been set and galleys have been pulled, and that your job is to read the galley proof for accuracy.

You might benefit from a few hints. The most effective proofreading requires two persons, one reading the copy aloud, noting punctuation, indention, dingbats and so on; and the other correcting proof with a red pencil. A quiet out-of-the-way room is indicated, and you and your partner might switch tasks from time to time, and take frequent short breaks. Although you are not asked to address widows or orphans in this assignment, or to deal with poor hyphenation or spaces left in the copy by faulty justification, note how many times in the short bit of copy in this assignment that such matters arise. Try to imagine how you would deal with them.

This assignment asks you to assume you have received your galley from a compositor. But remember that, with desktop publishing, you might find yourself being your own type composer and proofreader. Imagine your task if the printer you've contracted for the job asks that all copy be sent along on disk. In addition to making certain that your computer and the printer's computer can work together flawlessly, such an arrangement seems to require that you proofread your own work. In such situations, always generate a hard copy before proofing. You will find that proofreading on a computer screen is not as effective as you might wish. Try to use a laser printer in such instances; it will sharpen the copy and make your proofreading job easier. Proceed as you would if someone else had sent the proofs to you for correction. Try not to get caught in the flow of your perfect copy.

Proofread the following galley (by yourself) and hand it in. You will be evaluated on accuracy and on the correct use of the appropriate proofreading symbols, which you can find in virtually any printing or design textbook.

Manuscript

If all mankind minus one, were of one opinion, and
only one person were of the contrary opinion, mankind
would be no more justified in silencing that one person,
than he, if he had the power, would be justified in
silencing mankind. Were an opinion a personal possession
of no value except to the owner; if to be obstructed in
the enjoyment of it were simply a private injury, it
would make some difference whether the injury was
inflicted on a few persons or on many. But the peculiar
evil of silencing the expression of an opinion is, that
it is robbing the human race; posterity as well as
the existing generation; those who dissent from the
opinion, still more than those who hold it. If the
opinion is right, they are deprived of the opportunity
of exchanging error for truth; if wrong, they lose, what
is almost as great a benefit, the clearer perception
and livelier impression of truth, produced by its
collision with error.

<u>On Liberty</u>
John Stuart Mill

If mankind minus one, were of one opinion, and only one person were of a contrary opinion, mankind would be no more justified in silencing that person, than he, if he had the power, would be justified in silencing mankind. Were an opinion a personal possession of no value except to the owner: if to be obstructed in the enjoyment of it were simply a private injury, It would make some difference whether the injury was inflicted on few persons or on many. But the particular evil of silencing the expression of an opinion is, that it is robbing the human race; posterety as well as the existing generation; those who dissent from the opinion still more than those who hold it. If the opinion is right, they are deprived of the opportunity of exchanging error for truth; if wrong, they lose, what is almost as great a benefit, the clearer perception and livlier impression of truth, produced by its collision with error.

On Liberty
John Stewart Mill

GALLEY PROOF

___ O.K. as is

___ O.K. with changes

___ New proof after changes

_____
Signature

_____
Date

13 GRIDS
AND GRIDDING

OBJECTIVE   After completing this assignment, you should appreciate the value of developing a grid or structure for a projected layout before beginning work on virtually any graphic communication effort, but especially on a multipage effort. You will learn how to develop a page architecture for each effort you undertake after considering such matters as the client's wishes, budget, content, and audience.

TO HAND IN   Submit a grid for two facing pages for a garden catalog, and then, working on copies of the grid, find and paste into place appropriate art and text on a two-page spread. This will give you a fair idea of how well your grid functioned.

ASSIGNMENT BACKGROUND   At their simplest, page grids appear to be little more than a number of lines scribed on a layout sheet to form a series of horizontal rows and vertical columns. They are much more than this, however. The lines themselves and their intersections define the underlying structure or foundation of a page or spread and help direct placement of page elements. Grid lines establish page size, margins, alleys, and the dimension of type pages. They can be useful in accommodating special binding needs, the placement of page headers and footers, sidebars, photographs, and marginalia. Page grids make visible the rules a graphic communicator intends to follow in making his or her layouts. Grids force graphic communicators to confront important questions regarding the appearance of printed materials, such as trim and type page sizes and shapes as well as column arrangements on the page. The best ones suggest how to place typographic elements so layouts are both effective and pleasing to the target audience or so they showcase the content. Developing and using grids is fundamental to successful design. Grids, properly constructed and then followed, offer significant advantages and exact few costs. If used properly, they contribute order and continuity to both an individual page and to the publication as a whole. When the beginning designer follows a grid, he or she gains an advantage in meeting the challenge of bringing all of the elements in a layout into their appropriate relationships with one another.

Provision for gridding is built into many computer programs that offer electronic page or area composition, a further indication of their important nature. Few continuing publications do not rely on a grid system for laying out pages, and even veterans can benefit by developing grids for one-time printed pieces. Although lines that form grids are not normally printed in the final work, and so are not visible to the reader's eye, they strongly influence page construction and so affect how a layout succeeds in attracting and holding attention and transferring meaning.

Making a grid is, unfortunately, deceptively simple. They are easily created by drawing horizontal and vertical lines on what is to be a page area. Vertical grid lines generally define columns that will hold type and visual copy, and horizontal lines define other important places on a page, including the top and bottom of columns. But the lines cannot be placed randomly or haphazardly. Ideally, page grids emerge from thinking about a publication and its purpose, content, audience, and the intensity of audience interest in the content. They can also emerge from thinking about special printing or binding needs. At their best, grids incorporate tried and true principles of graphic communication. Although most beginners do not think much about grids when facing their first design tasks, they will soon come to see that intuition offers only limited help in solving real-world design and layout problems. This is especially true in electronic or desktop publishing, where elements can be easily placed and moved about on little more than a whim. In such situations, a clear plan or map, such as a grid provides, can help a beginning graphic communicator succeed in designing and laying out an annual report, a newsletter, direct mail appeal, or training manual. Once a suitable grid is produced, the graphic communicator can focus his or her energies on communicating necessary information. A good grid can reduce immeasurably that wasting of time and effort in getting all elements working together.

Gridding decisions not only help graphic communicators apply sound graphic principles, but they can help establish a personality for a printed work. This is especially true for consumer magazines. Try to imagine *Reader's Digest* as a 9 × 14 magazine, or *Vogue* as 4 × 6. Neither makes much sense. Try then to imagine two publications, each in A4 size. The grid for one indicates six or seven columns on a page. The second is a one-column format. Which format and grid do you think will more than likely be associated with an exciting variety of visual elements? Which with more thoughtful and contemplative content? Which do you think might be used for a fashion spread, for coverage of the Indianapolis 500, or for publication of a serious subject such as the biography of a U.S. president or presentation of the results of a medical forum?

Deciding on a grid scheme begins early in the process of designing printed works, and after one has been established (thoughtfully), there are advantages to following it. First, observing the rules forces discipline on a designer of a printed piece. After a while, readers, too, come to have expectations for the publication; they expect it to approach its content in a more or less consistent manner over time. The publication becomes comfortable to them. Because the graphic communicator exhibits discipline and members of the audience come to have consistent expectations, the graphic communicator can add drama to a layout very effectively merely by breaking a grid rule. For example, a dramatic photograph of an especially scenic location that is to run in a travel publication can be given greater magnitude by breaking the margin rule and having it run off the page (a bleed). Readers may not be able to say exactly why, but it is likely that they will react a bit more strongly to visual elements that break an unvaryingly and rigorously observed layout rule. This effect is possible only if one normally follows grid rules.

Deciding on a grid scheme can also save a good deal of time for a publication that has a deadline, because it forces decision making about the general appearance and the particular mode of presenting content to be made before the hustle and bustle of deadline day begins. And finally, a grid is helpful whenever more than one person is working on a publication, especially when the publication represents the work of a number of people separated by time and distance, as they often are in multinational corporations. The grid helps everyone know what is expected and provides clear directions for the achievement of agreed upon goals.

Recall that grids arise out of thinking about the publication, its reason for being, content, and audience. Generally, the most important concern in the journalistic media of newspapers and magazines is readability, although for some popular magazines, especially fashion magazines, the major concern might be creating visual excitement. For others, a major concern might be establishing page spaces that meet advertiser needs. But, generally, readability is a top concern. In such instances, one might expect to see a grid with columns that are appropriately wide for reading ease, given the typeface, type size, and leading chosen. Settling on a column width is a matter of shooting for a measure that yields good readability. For example, observing the rule that a line of type should contain about 40 characters sets the column width of a magazine fairly precisely. Very often, too, the selection of the amount of space used to separate columns of type (called, variously, *alleys* or *gutters*) comes to be the common spacing used between page elements throughout the publication. For example, if the alleys are 1 pica wide, the grid can be constructed to indicate that 1 pica of space should be used to separate each photograph from its cutline, and 1 pica should be used between the title and the byline, 1 pica between headers and footers and column material, perhaps double that to separate different items, and so on. Observing rules such as this also helps to establish continuity.

In a number of publications, the type size plus any leading is called the *line spacing* and it becomes the vertical measure for the page. Each line of copy, each photo, each element on the page must be placed on one of the resulting dimensional lines. This extremely precise and demanding grid goes by the name of *Swiss Grid*. It can be extremely effective in bringing order to pages that follow its rules. The orderliness of presentation suggests at a graphic level that the publication is taking an equally orderly, consistent, and serious look at happenings in its content area. The development of the Swiss Grid was spurred by some who thought partly to use the underlying precise mathematical nature of such a grid to diminish cultural and idiosyncratic personal expression in printed work. Designers who used such a grid could then concentrate solely on the content of communication without having to consider cultural and personal interference with the message. As a result, this type of grid might prove useful in producing printed works intended to cross or transcend cultural boundaries, a concern that has a good deal of appeal for international corporations such as IBM, Pizza Hut, McDonald's, and Kimberly Clark, each of which is represented in a number of nations.

Of course, the strongest criticism of gridding is that it forces a designer to place elements in a predetermined and rigid structure, thus stifling creativity and not allowing the designer to interpret content freely and craft a page that effectively communicates its meaning. This position, while not necessarily valid, has led designers to explore new directions in creating designs. Such efforts commonly are based on a rejection of the need for an underlying page structure throughout a publication in favor of a "do whatever has to be done" approach. Appropriate layouts for particular articles arise out of the designer's reading of the verbal and visual content of a specific article or feature and ways of making it graphically strong, as well as the designer's understanding of the audience and its immediate and particular needs. Grids go out the window. Nothing is permitted to hamper the exuberance, enthusiasm, and creativity that a trained designer should bring to bear in achieving the best solution to every problem posed. The emphasis shifts from orderliness to a focus solely on enhancing the relationships between and among elements in an individual spread, and carrying the results to the intended audience. Results can be wild, even disorganized. But, although this approach seems simple, it demands a good deal of sophistication on the part of the designer by requiring thoughtful attention to all variables, including content, graphic elements, audience interest, and design principles.

With the preceding in mind, it is time to take a look at the underlying grids of several publications that Americans know fairly well. These might include *Newsweek* or *Time, Vogue, The New Yorker, Better Homes & Gardens*, a young person's magazine such as *Seventeen*, and a local newspaper. Find a copy of each of five or six different magazines and leaf through their pages. Keep your eyes open and try to visualize the grid scheme of each publication. Note obvious differences among them. Keep in mind that the world of news does not generally require much in the way of flexibility of presentation and so grids for news publications tend to be straightforward and no-nonsense in nature. On the other hand, grids for magazines that hope to attract their audience by generating excitement, such as *Seventeen, GQ,* or *Maxim,* tend to be more complex, and this complexity offers a designer more choices in presenting content.

If you begin with the newspaper, you will likely find that its grid is based on six columns on the page, at least on the open news pages. You may note that the editorial pages seem to rely on a different grid scheme while the classified advertising pages have yet another. It is almost as though someone created a multiple grid scheme to meet diverse audience needs for news, comment, and advertising. It is easy to deduce why classified advertising page grids have 10 or 11 columns. Most newspapers sell this space by the column inch. There are many more column inches on an 11-column page than on a 6-column page, and so the 11-column page will produce more revenue for the newspaper than a page with fewer columns. On the other hand, the relatively wide columns on the open news pages are a good length for enhancing readability, and so the news page grid arises out of a concern that impatient and rushed readers be able to quickly learn what's news (the headlines also help a good deal).

As you continue to examine newspapers and magazines, you will also notice that most don't seem to have much space to waste and so their grids provide for narrow margins and alleys (the spaces between columns of type). Recall that books rely on progressive margins, with about half of the page taken up by margins. This luxury is not available to other forms of printed material, especially magazines and newsletters, which rely on what are called *functional margins*. Such margins are small and may be equal in size around the page.

ASSIGNMENT   When you have analyzed enough publications to give you a feel for their underlying grid structures, try your hand at creating a grid for a gardening booklet or catalog prepared by a seed company specializing in selling complete garden seed and plant packages. One collection offers flowers that bloom in succession from late spring until the first frost; one contains only heirloom varieties; another offers flowers designed to attract hummingbirds; another offers a patriotic motif, with only red, white, and blue flowers, all of which are in bloom around the beginning of July. Of course, gardeners want to know how their gardens will look when grown, how to identify individual plants in the collection, and how to plant the seeds. The graphic communicator will try capture in the booklet the excitement of spring planting and the beauty, color, and special nature of each garden. The company offers a total of 12 gardens, including butterfly, hummingbird, everblooming, patriotic, and so on. The company projects a 16-page self-cover publication.

Your assignment is to create an appropriate grid. In doing so, you might want to consider a number of questions. What content is expected by prospects to whom the booklet will be sent? What are other gardening publications offering? Will it help to ask several local gardeners what excites them? Anyone who has ever received a gardening publication knows that pictures of plants are prominently featured, along with a small amount of stirring copy describing the virtues of the particular cultivar, and a pricing guide. Very clearly, the most important aspect to this particular problem is presenting an exiting visual package of what buyers of any of the gardens can expect. Of course, most gardens will spread horizontally across the soil so the grid should offer the designer a grid scheme that allows for showcasing drawings, paintings, or photographs. On the other hand, some plants grow tall and demand a strong vertical space. Seeing large and colorful representations of the plants sparks interest in serious gardeners, and they can serve as a guide at planting time. Because there will be a variety of plants, each of them will need to be described and, presumably, a name or title for each garden will be featured as a title line.

Think the problem through, and then create and draw grids for two facing pages. The appearance of your publication is really pretty much up to you. But think. Make all appropriate decisions, including trim page size, margins and type page size, column widths, and so on. Try to anticipate problems that producing such a booklet might entail and address them with the grid. Be prepared to share your ideas with others. When you have completed your grids, make copies of them. Then collect colorful art, headlines, and text copy and paste up the page elements as you would have them appear. Try to find art copy of flowers, but if you can't, try to capture the feeling of flowers by using a good deal of color. The text does not have to make sense, but try to capture the weight and general appearance of the page elements that you would select for such a layout. When you have the pages pasted up, prop them up, move back 10 to 15 feet, and look at what you have done. Squint your eyes. What general flavor do you take away from your layout? What is its essential

character? Do you think it is the type of layout that a garden company might put together? Why, or why not?

   When you are satisfied, hand in your result.

ASSIGNMENT AIDS   Below are several examples of page grids.

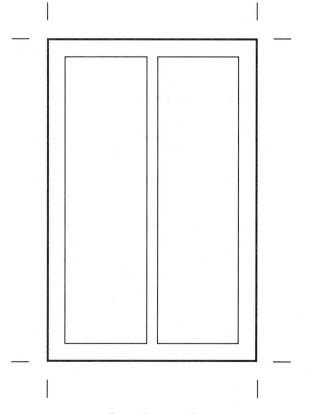

Two-column grid

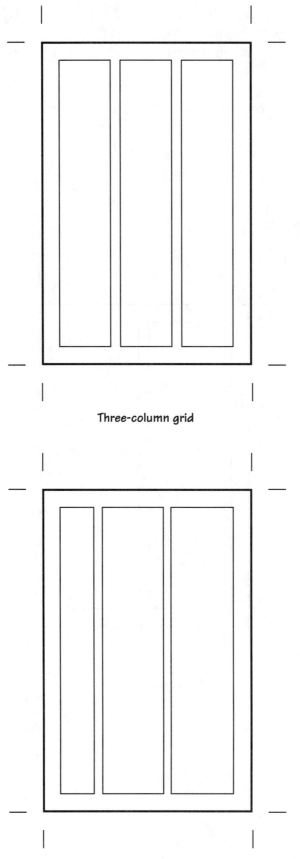

Three-column grid

Specialized grid

14 RÉSUMÉ

OBJECTIVE   This assignment challenges you to use your typographic and design skills to announce yourself as an important, newly minted graphic communicator about to burst onto the professional scene. Your résumé will provide prospective employers with a useful snapshot of you, your talents, and experiences, and its physical form will reveal to them the depth of your knowledge of typography and the informed use of space. It will be clear to all who receive it that you are a professional-in-becoming and destined to dominate the regional graphics scene. The résumé is a part of a more extensive project that will require your sustained attention as you design a personal stationery package, including an identity mark, letterhead, envelope, and business card to supplement your résumé.

TO HAND IN   Hand in a rough of your résumé, marked up, and a tentative type policy for your identity package. These will be evaluated, critiqued with you, and returned for reworking.

ASSIGNMENT   There are probably as many suggestions for what constitutes an ideal
BACKGROUND   résumé as there are résumé writers and those who receive them. Most educational institutions provide, through a placement or career office, a page or two of general guidelines that beginners can follow when crafting their first résumé. Some may provide one-on-one counseling. Professional organizations in your area might sponsor workshops. There are numerous library resources that can be consulted as well as advice columns covering résumés, interviews, and so on in the employment sections of many Sunday newspapers. In addition, most computer word-processing programs provide résumé templates that are very easy to use and that offer solid examples of this important document.

A suggestion common to virtually all guidelines for beginners is that pertinent experiences be grouped in blocks under one of a number of general headings, and that the headings be arrayed in an appropriate and logical order. Standard headings or categories include, in no particular order, career objectives, work experience, educational experience, awards and honors, extracurricular activities, special skills, and references. These categories can be moved about for a particular employer or to showcase special accomplishments, and they can easily be supplemented as needed.

Now is also the time when you will want to begin to think about a proper paper on which you wish your résumé printed. Paper selection is more important than you think. When a potential employer removes your résumé from its envelope, the paper is the tangible you. (The typeface and general appearance of the résumé add to the total impression.) If the paper is cheap and lightweight and feels unpleasant to the touch, some of that unpleasantness, felt unconsciously rather than intellectually, might be transferred to you. If the paper supports an opposite impression, you might benefit from it. If the paper, type, and ink are selected carefully, your résumé entries will leap off the page into the reader's eyes and brain. So, paper selection is important, although choosing a particular one from literally thousands of different kinds of paper in a wide variety of weights, finishes, and colors can be daunting. Keep in mind that you learned how to select suitable typefaces for particular jobs from thousands available, and selecting paper might not be any more difficult.

So how can you select the proper one? First of all, most paper companies and paper merchants supply sample books, and many printers stock them, too. A printer's knowledge of paper and its printing qualities can be helpful in pointing you in the right direction. In a pinch, look up entries in the Yellow Pages under paper distributors or paper manufacturers and get on the phone and start some detective work. Ask them to send you a few samples. If you can't obtain a sample book, go to a local office supply store and browse the paper section, trying to learn all you can. However you go about it, keep your eyes open and begin to develop a knowledge of this most important resource. Although the particular paper you intend to use does not have to be identified right now, be on the lookout for something suitable. When you run across a variety of paper you like, turn it in as an example, and your instructor can help you on the identification. As you develop your own resources, you will want to identify your choice of paper at least by name, paper grade, weight, size, color and manufacturer. Of course, you know enough to avoid dark colors that might interfere with readability and be difficult to copy on a standard copier. Convention dictates a white or very slightly off-white bond for a typical résumé, about 20-pound weight, in standard $8\frac{1}{2} \times 11$ size. You might want to consider experimenting with a metric size. These are more commonly found in Europe, but using such a size might be indicated if you plan to circulate your résumé to multinational companies.

Finally, you should be aware of an increasingly common, and disconcerting, employment practice. Some employers can now scan résumés they receive by means of optical character recognition (OCR) software and easily store and then retrieve the résumés using computer software. If an employer you approach has this type of system in place, it is conceivable that no single human being will study your résumé or appreciate the hard work that went into it, at least not until after it is flagged by a software filter. This changes radically the thrust of résumé design. For starters, you may want to use only very common typefaces, which are easily readable by OCR equipment; perhaps a simple sans serif such as Helvetica or Futura might be indicated. You might also want to select a larger typeface, again in deference to limitations in scanning programs. The common devices of underlining, italicizing, setting boldface, and using unusual capitalization schemes for emphasis may not be advisable, either, lest they interfere with character recognition.

A final chilling thought is that after your résumé is scanned and the information stored, the retrieval process probably entails looking for key words or word combinations. If this is true, you want to have some of those "golden words" in your résumé. You may be able to pick up some good ones from the position description in the advertisement to which you are responding. It may contain some of these must-use words. Use your imagination to identify other possibilities, such as *supervisor*, *manager*, or even *team player*. Keep this in mind as you build your résumé.

ASSIGNMENT   You can either craft a résumé from scratch or use this opportunity to polish your current one. If you have not begun to think about a résumé, probably the best advice is for you to review several of the resources available to you from those identified previously to create a résumé that seems comfortable for you. Your major graphic challenges are to select appropriate typography, to apply an appropriate typographic hierarchy, and to be careful to use the limited space on the page to present a clear and revealing verbal snapshot of yourself. When you have settled on your résumé content and given your ideas a form, mark it up using an overlay sheet and suggest a type policy for your identification package. Pay attention to your type selections, as they can say a good deal about you.

Use the following ideas as a minichecklist to work your way through after you have committed a tentative résumé to paper.

- *Content:* Are your career objectives, work and education experience, and honors/achievements clearly stated?

- *General appearance of page:* Is the page comfortably full, but not cramped? Does it appear to be light and airy or heavy and serious? Is it businesslike?

- *General approach to résumé layout:* Is your letterhead predominantly formal or informal? Is it a single column or have you decided to use multiple (usually two) columns to generate a little bit of excitement?

- *Consistent and appropriate grouping:* Have you collected similar experiences under the same heading? Do your categories of experience follow one another logically?

- *Consistency of spacing on page:* Are similar experiences grouped, are categories separated from one another by appropriate amounts of space, and is the spacing scheme applied consistently?

- *Consistency of typography:* Is your typography appropriate for a résumé? Appropriateness might be judged by your selection of type family, family branch, size, leading, and capitalization scheme.

- *Spelling and precision:* Have you checked and double-checked job titles, programs of study and academic course titles, computer program names, punctuation, and so on?

- *Style matters:* Is there a consistent style for content? Pay special attention to abbreviations and to the use of months and years to illustrate the lengths of tenure in all of your experiences.

15 STATIONERY PACKAGE: IDENTITY MARKS, LETTERHEADS, ENVELOPES, AND BUSINESS CARDS

OBJECTIVE Some graphic materials are produced so they will attract attention, shock, or otherwise engage an audience; others serve as an unobtrusive platform on which to place content and facilitate readability. The stationery package you are asked to produce for this longer-term assignment—a combination of identity mark, letterhead, envelope, and business card—must accomplish both purposes. It should have graphic power sufficient to grab its intended audience and showcase you, while simultaneously providing a platform that effectively highlights the message you wish to send. The envelope must meet appropriate postal regulations. This assignment will introduce you to some of these concepts and help you to develop your own special package.

TO HAND IN The first part of this multistep project is to hand in a number of thumbnails of your proposed identity mark, letterhead, envelope, and business card, accompanied by a type policy. After consultation with the instructor on all portions of this project, you will be given the go-ahead to complete roughs.

ASSIGNMENT BACKGROUND There is value in developing your own identity mark and stationery package. The brilliance of the components of such a package can be an effective means of exhibiting to potential employers some of your outstanding talents, in this case your graphic communication skills. When the components of this package, accompanied by your résumé, have been sent and received, an employer may find it impossible to resist hiring you. At the very least, if you are thoughtful in developing your package and if it is attractive and well-ordered, it may help set you apart from all the others.

A short word of caution is warranted. It would be foolish of you to imagine that you can sit down and in a relatively short time settle on your approach to your stationery package and complete its production. The discussion of this assignment is limited and abbreviated. The time allotted for completing it is woefully short. It might be best to look upon this assignment, discussion, and production as merely the beginning of a much longer process that might well take weeks if not months to complete.

Because you are not the first person to think seriously of creating your own identity mark and incorporating it into a stationery package, you should be able to find plenty of examples of good ones without too much trouble. Although most of the materials you run across probably were produced for corporate purposes, analyzing them can give you insights into their creation that, with modification, can be made applicable to your personal needs. Keep your eyes open. As with most graphics assignments, you do not have to reinvent the wheel with each new challenge. You should look each day with an appreciative eye at the numerous solutions to graphic problems you run across, and a number of such striking solutions should be accumulating in your swipe file. You can keep such a file current by collecting good examples and periodically reviewing them, both to familiarize yourself with them and to discard examples that exhibit techniques you have internalized or mastered. It may be fruitful to seek the opinions of professionals when you have a particular problem to solve. Talking with professionals in comfortable settings is one good reason for joining a professional organization active in your city or region. You should also get in the habit of browsing in a library or visiting nearby agencies or design studios to get a feel for what is current. However you go about generating your ideas, when you have settled on a good one, it is time to begin the project.

A good first step to take centers around a process called *visualization*. This is a specific and particular process, the components of which force you to consider the building blocks of your assignment. Visualization is a four-step process:

- Selecting the proper symbols to represent and project your message

- Deciding how many graphic elements will be required

- Deciding the relative importance of elements and determining how best to attract attention to this part of the message

- Determining the path you would like a recipient to take through your message

For this assignment, you will have to determine which verbal and visual symbols you wish to represent who you are and what you have to offer. Careful and systematic consideration can lead you to make good type decisions and suggest visual copy, use of color, and so on. Generally, the more elements you include, the greater the potential for creating excitement. At the same time, too many elements on a sheet can project a feeling of clutter. And, while including fewer elements tends to project a serious tone, that path may run the risk of boring recipients. Deciding on the number of elements to be included in a project such as this brings up the practical matter of size. How many elements can be fitted comfortably onto a business card that is only $3\frac{1}{2} \times 2$ inches? On the face of an envelope or at the top or side of a letterhead? You might have to include a home and a work address, home and work telephones, e-mail address, fax numbers, and so on. Can the elements you select withstand the enlargement and reduction called for as you move from letterhead page size to business card size? Determining the relative importance of elements requires you to consider the principle of contrast to assure that the appropriate symbol has been emphasized so that it will be the first one processed by those exposed to it. Finally, you would like to strongly suggest, graphically, that recipients of your materials proceed in a certain order through them, perhaps by reading the letter first and then filing your business card for future reference. Try to imagine how the elements can be arranged so that this process flows smoothly and naturally.

Identity Marks. Your identity mark should be coordinated, in tone and typography, with the other elements of the stationery package. Remember that your identity symbol will both identify you and be a design element of the package, so it must relate strongly to you and be an appropriate part of an attractive presentation. All parts of the package are important and should be coordinated carefully.

As you develop your identity mark, you might want to reflect on the long and glorious history such marks have had. Some of them have endured a good long time and continue to speak to us today. Some examples are those used by publishers (called colophons) and papermakers (watermarks); the Christian cross; the Golden Arches; the revolving, striped barber pole; and the Nazi swastika. Numerous others are familiar, having been developed for use in modern advertising campaigns or for other corporate initiatives.

The use of trademarks and service marks probably dates from medieval times, and they likely were, at first, required by authorities in order to pin blame on producers of shoddy merchandise. Marks seem to have taken on a new function recently, as a type of badge that bestows status on the user of products. Some of these marks include Nautica, Polo, and Calvin Klein. A great industry has grown and prospered in meeting the needs of those who would like to have a professionally designed logo or mark that gets across the essence of that person, organization, industry, or business, and that is recognized by a wide variety of individuals, including customers, shareholders, wholesalers, dealers, and the public at large.

The power of an identity mark, or logo, lies in its ability to be recognized and its message understood, preferably instantaneously.

There is also the matter of the ease with which it can be modified for incorporation into a total identity and marketing program for a person, business, or organization. Such widespread uses might include:

- Business cards for its personnel

- Forms for conducting business (with customers, shareholders, wholesalers, and so on)

- Direct mail, letterheads, stationery, envelopes

- Signage for outdoor advertisements, vehicle identification, and uniform insignia

- Customer, employee, and service manuals

- Advertising and other promotional materials

- Mailing labels, packaging, and a thousand other uses.

There is also the matter of modification if the sponsoring organization changes, or if social changes require re-analysis of its role. Of course, really well-known logos, such as Coca-Cola or GE, may be so successful that altering them is virtually unthinkable. However, several examples of logos that did change spring to mind. There was Aunt Jemima, who was portrayed on the boxes of pancake and waffle mix as an archetypal slave cook; she became a modern African-American woman. It also is interesting to note the evolution of Betty Crocker. Changes were made to her facial features, her hairstyle, and to the clothes she wore as she successively trudged, bounced, and strode through American history, from the years of the Great Depression to today.

In a fast-paced world where each of us can expect to receive more than a thousand messages each day, having an identification mark that leads to easy recognition is certainly a plus. Such a mark clearly states who you are, what you stand for, and what services you provide or goods you produce. All of this must be accomplished with limited tools, including only type, visual copy, and color.

There are, however, some characteristics of good identity marks, including:

- Simplicity

- Distinctiveness

- Functionality

Most marks today have been stripped to the barest of essentials and are little more than shape, line, point, tone, and texture. Over the years many have gone from representation to abstraction, and in the process have been stripped of ornamentation. Distinctiveness is more than a graphic problem of competing with others; it can be a legal matter. Companies go to extraordinary lengths to develop distinctive symbols for their exclusive use. There is a body of law that protects their use of such marks, and owners of popular marks hire lawyers to search out and deal with infringements (the Disney company is especially active in this regard). The law requires that the developers of such identifiable marks protect their own use by aggressively pursuing others who use identical or substantially similar marks without permission.

Finally, the best marks are easily capable of being put to a wide variety of uses; they can be printed on paper; projected on a television screen; enlarged on outdoor advertisement sheets; copied and faxed; enlarged and reduced; put on envelopes and letterheads, soup cans and boxes, and rubber stamps; and, in the case of Batman, projected onto the clouds.

Stationery. Often an identity mark becomes an integral part of a letterhead. The letterhead itself is especially important because it may be the first and perhaps the only contact a person has with an organization. Although letterheads are not necessarily impersonal, they have a predominantly institutional purpose. At the same time, the business card also serves this institutional function, although it is more personal because it is handed from one person to another, face to face, and in a manner that often encourages conversation.

Generally, letterheads are charged with two major functions:

- Making a statement about the message sender

- Showcasing letter content by making it easy to read

The type styles, sizes, and colors that you select for your letterhead, and the arrangement of elements on the page set the stage for receipt of the message by creating a frame of reference for the reader. That frame of reference determines the approach the viewer will take to the company, and, by extension, the message. A current term for framing these days is *spin*. The idea of spin is that if you can determine the frame of reference for the reception of a message, you have, many times, won any arguments you advance in that context. In the case of this project, you are using type and space in your layout to showcase yourself, proclaim your competence, and argue for serious consideration as a good person to hire. Envelopes and business cards supplement that basic argument.

There are two general approaches to laying out a letterhead: formal and informal. Formal balance generally requires that you array all elements on the page around a vertical center axis. Informal balance allows you to use other arrangements so long as the whole is balanced. Informality can help you to project energy and confidence in yourself, while formality hints at the serious nature of what you have to offer, your stability, and your attention to order. Neither approach is appropriate under all circumstances, and selecting one over the other for any specific application requires careful thought.

The same is true for using colored and textured papers. Both are strong variables and can be important means of adding individuality to your package, making it stand out. Because color is such a strong element, paper colors can help establish or reflect your personality and character and might even hint at your qualifications for the position you are seeking. Red connotes activity, while blue connotes peace and quiet. The color of paper can help get across the basic view you have of yourself. For example, if the job you are applying for involves working with others in a team setting, a paper that runs to a warm off-white (toward the beige, tan, and brown) might help establish your warmth and conviviality; a cooler off-white (toward the blues and greens) might hint more effectively at your technical competence and expertise.

Because no letterhead arrives blank, setting margins is important so the letter is inviting and appears to be easy to read. Recall that establishing the width of margins on a page creates line lengths for the type, and line lengths are closely related to readability. And make no mistake, you want your letter and résumé to be read, thoroughly. The easier you make them to read, the greater the chances are that they will be given the time and attention they deserve.

There are three popular sizes for letterheads. The first is $8\frac{1}{2} \times 11$. There is a size termed *monarch* at $7\frac{1}{4} \times 10\frac{1}{2}$, and a half-sheet is $5\frac{1}{2} \times 8\frac{1}{2}$. Currently, the most commonly used size is $8\frac{1}{2} \times 11$. Access to monarch size is often granted only to those higher up in an organization, at the corporate level. Half-sheets can be useful for brief messages. Although the United States has not converted wholeheartedly to the metric system, many other nations rely on it and the U.S. is going to have to adopt it sooner or later. Many of us have received a letter that seems to be oddly proportioned, deeper than most and a bit narrower. This is a metric-sized sheet. Even if you don't select a metric size for this project, you should begin to learn about its use. The metric series is simple to learn. It is based on a basic size, A0, which is one square meter of paper, with the sides in a ratio of 1:1.414 (the square root of 2). The next smaller size is A1, which is one-half square meter of paper (again with the sides in the ratio of 1:1.414); A2 is half of A1 and so on. In this scheme of halving, the sizes retain their 1:1.41 ratio of width to depth. There is also a C-series, for envelopes, so that an A4 sheet fits into a C4 envelope and so on.

If nothing else, the metric scheme brings some degree of order to the world of paper, which is characterized by an incredible variety of common paper and envelope types and sizes. When you select paper for printing your stationery package, you will want to have an appropriately sized envelope in the same stock as the letterhead. The printer can arrange for envelopes at the same time you are ordering the rest of your package. Traditionally, business envelope sizes have been identified by numbers, such as #10, #9, and so on. The most common size is a #10, which is about 9½ inches on the long dimension and 4⅛ inches on the short dimension. In the envelope world, size in inches is always the depth first and then the width—the opposite of the usual means of identifying paper or publication trim page sizes. As you arrange for envelopes, you should also consider postal regulations lest you select a nonstandard envelope and incur a surcharge based on an unusual size, shape, thickness, or weight. It's usually best to stick to common sizes. If you are uncertain, take an example to the local post office and ask.

Business cards are small, and there is no room on them for much in the way of a personal message. They are a little bit like billboards in that they hold a limited message. Even though they aren't meant to carry much in the way of messages, many people find themselves writing on the back of them as they hand them to others; perhaps it's a home telephone number, the number of a colleague, a meeting date and time, and so on. Business cards must do double and triple duty these days, with lines for snail-mail address, e-mail and Internet addresses, telephone numbers (perhaps home and work and even cellular), and fax numbers. Whatever is included on them, when they are put in another person's Rolodex, they become your presence in another's office, so a good deal of care should be exercised in their creation.

As with other materials in this package, business cards can appear formal, dignified, informal, friendly, and so on. They can be outrageous, or cool, if that is the image you hope to project. Because they are small they are perfect candidates for a single typeface, which might be sans serif so the information on them jumps off the card.

Remember that, as for many other things in the graphic arts, there is a standard business card size, about 3½ × 2 inches, and it is generally not wise to use a different size without a good reason. That said, realize that vertical cards are becoming more acceptable. An odd-sized business card may not fit into a standard Rolodex, or it may offend a person who likes all of the cards he or she receives to square up on all edges. Such a person would definitely not appreciate a card that was one-eighth of an inch wider than every other card in the collection, and would probably pitch out a card with a deckled edge. On the other hand, an odd-sized card is different, stands out, and might attract extra attention. You have to choose, based on who you are and what you are trying to accomplish in your dealings with others. Generally, cards are printed on a relatively heavy stock, and they may utilize thermography, die-cutting, embossing, or other special treatments. Ask the printer what is possible. But remember that the card should not be wildly different from the rest of your package in tone or physical characteristics.

That, in a nutshell, is something you should know about identification marks. Your assignment over the next few weeks is to develop a personal mark and then include it on a letterhead, envelope, and business card.

ASSIGNMENT   Begin by working on preliminary drawings (thumbnail size) of your mark, letterhead, envelope, and business card. Hand in at least a dozen thumbnails. After discussion with the instructor, move the best of them along to the rough stage, and hand in roughs of all components in the package when you have completed them.

ASSIGNMENT AID   Following is a drawing of the four common sizes of letterheads.

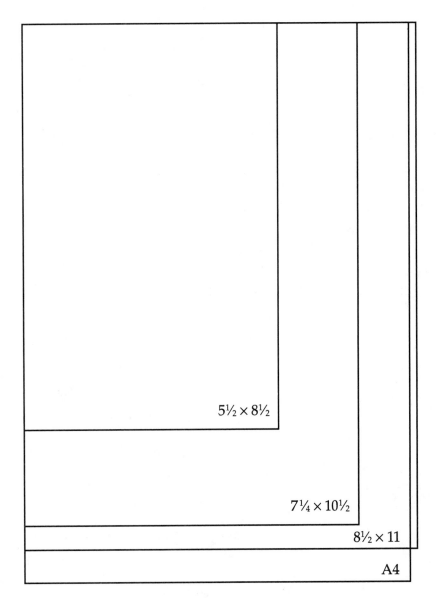

$5\frac{1}{2} \times 8\frac{1}{2}$

$7\frac{1}{4} \times 10\frac{1}{2}$

$8\frac{1}{2} \times 11$

A4

Common letterhead sizes

16 COPYFITTING

OBJECTIVE This assignment explains the mystery of determining how to predict accurately how much space copy will take up when it is typeset. Knowing how to copyfit both display and body sizes of type can facilitate design and layout chores by giving you important information about your layouts before you go to the time and expense of setting your copy into type. This assignment will also help you to understand how to go about assigning writing projects to others so that their copy, when typeset, will take up the precise amount of space in your publication that you planned upon. Knowing such things allows you to work on layout and design problems while waiting for the copy to be sent to you. Fitting copy is a skill that you are likely to draw upon often in your professional career. Knowing how to do so will result in greater personal satisfaction and less professional annoyance as you go about producing printed materials.

TO HAND IN Hand in the unit counts of several display lines and complete several copyfitting problems.

ASSIGNMENT BACKGROUND Making certain that the text you have written will fit into the space you've allocated for it is called *copyfitting*. The problem was nicely phrased in a textbook by Craig Denton: "Editors and art directors share a nightmare . . . that copy . . . (is) twice as long as space will allow or stops short and leaves one extra (un)planned page to fill." Copyfitting can give you peace of mind that this particular nightmare will not visit you. The problem that copyfitting solves confronts every graphic communicator sooner or later, but it need not be a problem if he or she learns how it is done. Learning it may not be a picnic, but in the long run, knowing how to copyfit is a stress reliever.

A minor difficulty is that several types of copyfitting exist side by side. Knowing when to use each is important. Generally, there are two applications of copyfitting:

- For display-sized type

- For body or text type

One might also want to divide copyfitting of text material or body copy into two kinds, based largely on which medium is applying the process, newspapers or most other printed media.

- A newspaper version of copyfitting is acceptably precise and can be accomplished quickly.

- Character-count copyfitting yields more precise information and is used for books and magazines.

Newspaper-type copyfitting is simple to apply and yields acceptable results with a minimum of time and fuss. This is in keeping with a newspaper's need for speed and to close out pages regularly in the newspaper cycle and send them to the back shop to be readied for printing. In its simplest form, the need for copyfitting occurs when an editor assesses the news value of, say, a political debate, and assigns a reporter to cover it and come back to the newsroom with a story that will take up about 15 column inches of the next day's news hole. The editor has obviously determined the event is worth a 15-inch space on a page. In the editor's mind, longer news stories are needed to signal more significant news and shorter stories usually indicate news of less significance. Most reporters, after only a day or two on the job, learn to determine roughly how much to write when given this kind of assignment, although it is not intuitive. The calculation involved is so simple that anyone can quickly learn to do it. For example, beginning reporters soon learn that if they set the line length in their word processing programs at 6 inches, there is a predictable, if loose, relationship between the amount of copy appearing on their monitor screens and the number of column inches their stories will take up when they are set into type. For example, they might come to learn that if they crank out four lines of copy, they will take up 1 column inch of newspaper space when typeset. Alternatively, they might come to realize that for every page they fill in their word-processing program, the typeset version will take up a certain number of column inches on the newspaper page. Anyone can learn to write his or her story and then count the number of lines or pages of copy written and divide by the appropriate figure.

Of course, when the editor places the article in the layout, he or she will have to add to it the number of column inches taken up by the headline and other space-using material such as subheads, bylines, pull quotes, and so on. If the story runs a little bit long, the layout or back shop staff is often able to make room on the page for that extra little bit, or may send the story to be cut. If the story is a little bit short, the layout staff might put in a small house ad, or a short bit of copy submitted by a charitable organization.

An alternative scenario, using a slightly different approach involves a beat reporter who writes a story he or she hopes will interest the public enough to begin a public policy debate. The reporter is striving hard to tell the story and is not under orders to produce a story of a particular length. When it is finished, however, space for it has to be allocated, and the editor inquires how much space to allow.

Now a second means of determining space, perhaps a bit more accurate than counting lines, comes into play. Most word-processing programs can provide information about the number of characters that have been written. Some newsroom computers have programs that tell precisely how many column inches every story will take up when typeset. In such cases, all the work is done. Just write a story and look to see how many picas of depth or column inches have to be reserved to hold it. But if such a program is not installed, the reporter can still complete the task easily. For example, if a reporter knows that a column inch can hold, on the average, 200 typeset characters, he or she can count the number of characters, including punctuation and spaces, in 10 column inches, add the total, and divide by 10 to learn the average. So, if it is 200, and if he or she has written 2,200 characters, the reporter can easily determine that the story is about 11 column inches (2,200 characters ÷ 200 = 11 inches). Similarly, if an editor requests a 15-inch story, and a reporter has written 3,500 characters, the reporter knows that he or she has to cut about 500 characters from the story (15 × 200 = 3,000). If he or she has written 2,700 characters, 300 more must be produced, or, alternatively, the editor will use a pull quote, a filler, a house ad, or some other device to fill the extra space. The virtue of this kind of copyfitting is that it can be done almost without thinking and yields fairly accurate results.

A second type of newspaper copyfitting, called *unit-count copyfitting*, involves the special case of fitting display-type-sized headlines into a given space, usually one, two, or three columns wide. Writing headlines is governed by several rules. For example, headlines must not only adequately relate to readers the meaning of the story and provide a measuring stick by which the importance of the story can be gauged, but they must aid in the design of the page so that it is inviting and not confusing. This means that headlines should not lap over the edges of the type columns into the margins on either side of the column of type, or be so long that they butt up to other headlines in other columns and thus cause reader confusion. They should fit a space nicely, but not be too long.

Unit-count copyfitting is useful in fitting display type to a space without having to go to the trouble of first setting the headline into type. It is useful not only for newsroom work, but also for advertising, pamphleteering, newsletters, and all sorts of printed material. It is a system based on allocating space for each and every character. Some characters take up little space (*I, f, l, t*) and some take up a good deal of space (*W, M, Q*), and the system accommodates this in a rough way by assigning a number of units to each letter, numeral, and punctuation mark. The number of units range from a half unit for skinny letters and some punctuation to two units for wider characters. And because each publication has its own type policy, it develops its own unit system to accommodate its particular type and spacing needs.

Usually a newspaper will provide a sheet, or headline schedule, on which all possible headline styles in all possible type sizes are listed, and all unit counts are included. Although the specifics vary, the basic system stays the same:

- Allow 2 units for the capitals *M* and *W*.

- Allow 1½ units for all other capitals, except allow one count for *I* and *J*.

- Allow 1 unit for lower-case letters, except for *f, l, i, t, j,* and, perhaps, *r*.

- Allow 1½ units for *m* and *w*, numerals, and some punctuation.

- Numerals and other punctuation are assigned whatever number of units is appropriate.

After you have written your headline, you can then easily count the number of units it contains, and if it is too long or too short to fit in the allocated space, it can be rewritten or otherwise altered so it does fit.

This part of this exercise requires you to count the units in each of the following headlines. Write the unit counts next to the headlines. Remember, however, that you are counting only line by line. It is the number of units in any single line that determines whether that particular line will fit into the space allocated and not the total count in, say, a three-line headline.

Disaster declared in flooded areas

This headline count is _____.

I-43 hassle
may be
taste of future

This headline count is   1. first line   _____.

                                    2. second line   _____.

                                    3. third line   _____.

Budget committee OKs $317 million income tax cut

This headline count is
1. first line ____.
2. second line ____.
3. third line ____.

Character-count copyfitting of body copy is the most accurate system because it accounts for every space and character. It takes into account the fact that when characters are typeset, each takes up a particular amount of space, unlike characters generated on a typewriter or in Courier typeface in a word-processing program, in which all characters take up an equal amount of space. In character-count copyfitting, the longer the manuscript the better the system works. Being able to accomplish character-count copyfitting is a valuable tool in book and magazine publishing. It is relatively easy because each manufacturer of type (metal, photographic, or digital) provides a single number that represents on the average the number of characters of that typeface, in that size and family branch, and so on that will fit into a pica of space along a line. These figures are widely published and readily available. So when a graphic communicator receives a long book manuscript and wants to be able to plan for its production, he or she can do character-count copyfitting and determine pretty closely how many pages the manuscript will take up when it is typeset. This helps your planning and may allow you to avoid charges for alterations that have to be made after the book has been typeset and you find that you have to edit it, thereby wasting the time and money it took to set the material that you now must cut.

Character-count copyfitting is fairly simple and straightforward. First you determine how many characters there are in a manuscript. Then, one logical path of inquiry requires you to determine how many characters can be fitted onto a page of typeset material, and then to determine how many pages will be needed to hold the entire manuscript. Once this is known, you can deal with a printer or a paper merchant with confidence, knowing precisely how many pages a given manuscript will take up. Armed with that information, you and the printer can determine how much paper and press time will be needed to print the work as well as costs of distribution and so on. Once those costs are known, you can estimate fairly closely the cost of the entire project. That can be very helpful at budget time when you have to determine which printed materials will be generated during the next budget cycle and their approximate costs. As always in the graphic arts, the more one knows, the more flexibility and freedom one has.

A common character-count copyfitting problem, for example, requires a graphic communicator to determine how much space a manuscript (ms.) will require when it is set in type. Perhaps it is a book or an article. For our purposes, assume that you've arranged for a freelancer to write an extensive article on health care and that the article is now sitting in front of you, in the form of a pile of pages or on a computer disk. You want to be able to determine accurately how much space the article will require before it is set in type. You can proceed in the following manner.

1. Mark up your typewritten manuscript (type, size, and so on. If you have a continuing publication, your type policy dictates the mark-up for you).

2. Count the number of characters in the manuscript (all characters, numerals, spaces, punctuation). Often this is a matter of asking the writer to include this figure, or you can boot up your computer and learn this by inserting the disk and getting that information directly. You can also do an acceptable job, if you have a hard copy, by counting the average number of characters in a line and multiplying by the number of lines in the manuscript.

3. Look up in an appropriate source the number of characters that can be fitted into a pica width of typeset material. This is often published information, or you can ask the compositor or printer for it. You know all the variables involved because you did the mark-up on the copy.

4. Determine how many characters can be fitted into a line of typeset material by multiplying the character per pica figure you learned in step 3. by the number of picas in the line. Again, it was your decision as to how wide, in picas, the lines were to be, so you know this figure.

5. Divide the total number of characters in the entire manuscript by the number of characters that will fit on a single line. The result is the number of lines that will be required to hold the manuscript (round up to the next number of lines if there is a fractional part of a line).

6. Determine how many total inches will be needed to hold the typeset manuscript by multiplying the number of lines that will be required by the number of points each line is deep (this is the *line spacing figure*, which is defined as the point size of type plus any leading). This will give you the total number

of points of depth you will need to hold all the lines of type that are needed. Then divide the result by 72 to learn how many column inches you will have to allow for.

7. Divide the column inches that can be held on a page into the total number of column inches you determined in step 6, and that will give you the total number of pages to plan for. Remember that each sheet has two sides, front and back, so each page is backed by another page.

Another common copyfitting application can be used to determine how much copy needs to be written to fill a predetermined copy block. Let's say that you have settled on a layout scheme for an advertisement. You plan on a full page in a periodical. You want to include a photograph and you've decided on its size and placement using your photoscaling skills. You have already told your photographer what you hope to achieve with the art, and its allocated size, so he or she can get busy. You've decided on a headline and mentally placed it in your layout. The rest of the space is for the copy, and you measure the proposed copy block's depth and width. It's now time for you to tell the copywriter how much copy to write to fill the remaining space. There are some simple steps you can follow for that also:

1. Decide on your mark-up (often for advertising copy it will be a larger type than you normally use, perhaps even a small display type size, or at least a rather large-sized body type).

2. Determine the number of characters that can be fitted into a line by multiplying the characters per pica (you've learned this from a table or asked your printer) by the picas per line.

3. Determine the number of lines by multiplying the depth in inches of the copy block you have chosen by 72 points (in an inch) and then dividing the result by the number of points a line will take up (point size + leading). The result will be the number of lines in the block(s).

4. Multiply the number of characters in a line by the number of lines that will fit into the depth to learn how many characters your copywriter will have to write to fill the space.

There are several useful formulas that can help you with such problems. To determine how much space a manuscript will require when typeset, use the following formula:

• Characters per line = characters per pica × picas per line.

• Total lines = total characters in the ms. divided by characters per line.

- Depth of copy = lines × points per line divided by 72 is the number of column inches the copy will require.

To determine how many characters to write to fill a given space in a layout, use the following formula:

- Characters per line = characters per pica × picas per line.
- Lines = depth in inches × 72 points per inch divided by points per line.
- Total characters = characters per line × number of lines.

If you follow these formulas and think your problem through, you should have little trouble with copyfitting. Practice will help you perfect this skill. Try the problems below for starters. First see if you can complete your work before looking at the answer, which follows.

Assume you have received a manuscript in hard copy form. You have before you 218 pages of copy. You determine that with about 60 characters in a line, and with 24 lines on a page, each page holds 1,440 characters, and with 218 pages, the manuscript contains 313,920 total characters. Assume you have chosen a type and size that the manufacturer assures you has a character per pica figure of 2.6. The type is 10 point, and you intend to lead it one point, so each line will require 11 points of depth. You have determined to use a 6 × 9 page size, with progressive margins as follows: bottom, 1½ inches; outside, 1 inch; top, 1 inch; inside, ¾ inch.

How many total pages will you have to account for to contain this manuscript? Hint: Draw out your trim page as a first step and then enter the type page in the space and place the measurements of both clearly on your drawing.

Apply the formulas, as follows.

1. Characters per line = characters per pica × picas per line:

$$2.6 \times (4\tfrac{1}{4} \text{ inches} \times 6)$$

$$2.6 \times 25.5 = 66.3$$

2. Total lines required to hold the copy = total manuscript characters ÷ characters per line:

$$313,920 \div 66.3 = 49,828 + \text{ or } 49,829$$

3. Total column inches required to hold the copy = lines × the points each line will require:

$$49,829 \times 11 = 548,119 \text{ points} \div 72 = 7,612.76 \text{ column inches}$$

4. Total pages the manuscript will require when typeset = the total number of column inches required to hold the manuscript copy ÷ the column inches each page will hold:

7,612.76 ÷ 6.5 inches per page = 1,171.19 pages
(a page turner, we hope)

If this seems to be a whole lot of pages, it is. You know that it is the job of the graphic communicator to read the audience and present messages in a form that will appeal to audience members. Add to that knowledge the idea that part of this appeal is the price of the work, which must be attractive, just as the appearance of the work must be attractive. If, after the graphic communicator checks with paper companies and printers to determine costs for such an extensive work, the client determines the cost is too high (perhaps the amount of paper required will push the cost of the project beyond the reach of potential readers), the graphic communicator can make limited adjustments to the copy in an attempt to reduce the number of pages. Strategies that should be considered include:

- Using a more condensed typeface so more characters can be fitted into a given space

- Using a smaller type size

- Reducing or eliminating leading

- Reducing margin space (which would both lengthen the lines and increase the number of lines on a page

Of course other changes might be made, but these tend to be the more fruitful in circumstances such as these. A graphic communicator, especially one who has some journalism training, would also want to consider tighter editing or asking the author take steps to reduce the word count. However it all turns out, the possibilities for change, and even the need for change, are meaningless until copyfitting is completed for the manuscript. Although you may not need to copyfit every day you are on the job, knowing how to do it might just save a good deal of embarrassment someday, and so it should be mastered.

Finally, another use of copyfitting presents itself when your client is committed to a particular layout for one reason or another, and he or she won't budge when you suggest changes. The client plans include a layout space allocated for copy, and now it is up to you to fill it (you have a good copywriter available, of course). The question now is, how many characters have to be written to fill the space? Assume this is your problem for the day. You have already been told the typeface must be 14 points, unleaded, also said to be "set solid." You learn that the type has a character per pica figure of 2.0. The copy block is 7 inches wide and 5 inches deep. How can you determine the number of characters your copywriter must write?

Conceptually, you would like to know how many characters can be fitted into a line, and then how many lines will fit into the space. When you multiply the two, you have your answer. Using the formula, we have

1. Characters per line = characters per pica × picas per line

    characters per line = $2.0 \times (7 \times 6) = 84$

2. Lines = total points of depth ÷ the points each line requires

    5 inches × 72 = total points of depth = 360

    360 ÷ 14 points per line = 25.71 lines

Perhaps you see the problem that has arisen. How can we have 25 lines plus another .71 line? That .71 of a line would be likely be enough to hold the ascenders and much of the x-height, but it certainly would not allow readers to know what the descenders looked like. So, we will either have to take it away, in which case we will plan on less than a 5-inch copy block, or we will have to add another .29 line and plan on a little bit more than a 5-inch-deep copy block. Most of us would add the extra little bit so we could write a little more copy to accomplish our task, so let's do that. That would give us 26 lines. To go on:

3. Characters per line × lines = total characters

    84 × 26 = 2,184 characters

So you can tell your copywriter to write 2,184 characters.

ASSIGNMENT   Complete the following problems and hand them in. Show all work.

- Assume you have a copy block 5 inches wide and 3 inches deep. You are using an 11-point typeface, leaded one point. Its character per pica figure is 3.0. How many characters must be generated in order to be sure of filling the copy block?

- You have received a manuscript for publication consisting of 224,396 characters. You intend to set this on a smallish page,

$5\frac{1}{2} \times 8$, with functional margins of $\frac{1}{2}$ inch all around the page. You will rely on a readable 9-point type, and because your intended audience is college-age readers, you feel that you can get along without leading. How many pages will be required to hold this manuscript? The character per pica figure is 3.8. Remember to draw out a page and assign margins so that you can see the dimensions of the type page.

17 SELF-GUIDED TOUR BROCHURE AND SIGNAGE

OBJECTIVE This assignment requires you to work with another person to conceive and carry to completion a relatively common graphic communication project: a self-mailing, two-fold brochure. This assignment may help you to appreciate the need to draw on the individual strengths of your team's members and forge agreements in advance of production on content and appearance of the work as well as on a fair division of labor. In addition, your team will develop signage appropriate to your tour.

Because an emphasis is placed on teams moving to completion by establishing a realistic and orderly work flow, there are intermediate steps built into this assignment, including submission of a written statement of what art and copy will have to be generated, creation of thumbnails, and the presentation of a relatively finished rough. Signage will progress through the same steps, beginning with thumbnails. Reasonably well-crafted roughs of the publication and the signage are the final outcomes for this project.

TO HAND IN Several intermediate assignments will culminate in a rough of the folder and another of two signs. You will have one week for each of the following steps:

- Selection of a tour site and a rationale for the brochure, and a tentative written statement of what art and copy will have to be generated, including division of labor on copy generation and design

- Thumbnails for the brochure and signage and generation of copy and art

- Art and text for both brochure and signage

- Roughs for brochure and signage.

ASSIGNMENT BACKGROUND An increasing number of organizations, including museums, zoos, botanical gardens, and even towns and cities, have adopted the idea of offering self-guided tours. Some offer little more than a single sheet with a rough map printed on one side. Other publications are a bit more attractive and useful. Generally, there are two distinct approaches to creating such guides. In one, users are led along a clearly marked path, leaving it to them to react to and interpret the significance of what they are seeing. Another approach is to call out special items for the reader, often presenting them in the form of photographs or drawings, accompanied by explanations. This adds a visual dimension that helps visitors recognize landmarks on the tour as they move along. Sites of interest along the route are often identified with small plaques or signs, which may have a distinctive design or color, so they stand out from the background. This can be very effective. In even more sophisticated presentations, a visitor may be given special key to insert in small boxes at points along the way, usually fastened to a post or pole, which activates a tape player. A recorded message reveals more about the site, which requires coordination of audio and printed communications.

ASSIGNMENT   The subject of this assignment is up to you; your project can be designed to help visitors to a local park, downtown area, a library, a government agency's quarters, a neighborhood, a sewage treatment plant, and so on. Select a place about which you already have some knowledge and interest so you will not have to do an inordinate amount of research before you begin.

Teams are responsible for producing both verbal and visual copy, the latter using standard or electronic cameras or scanning already existing art. You may use stock or clip art or other prepared materials without limit. Part of the challenge of this assignment is to find visual materials appropriate to your needs or to create them yourselves.

Draw on your typographic and visual skills and knowledge of design to produce an attractive brochure and accompanying signage. Two signs are required, and it is strongly suggested that your team develop a suitable visual theme to be carried through both the publication and the signage. The components of the package should send a consistent, positive, and enthusiastic message. You may use any colors you wish, so long as you specify them properly on your layout (4-color, PMS spot color, duotone, and so on).

The pamphlet must be printed or copied on an $8\frac{1}{2} \times 11$ flat sheet, folded twice, to $3\frac{2}{3} \times 8\frac{1}{2}$. It is a self-mailer. Signage must be no larger than 13 by 9 inches and no smaller than 9 by 6 inches, horizontal or vertical.

A good general approach to completing this assignment is to make a number of decisions about the content of your brochure early on. For example, you should select symbols you think can best represent your ideas, determine how many symbols are needed to communicate your ideas fully, determine the amount of emphasis each element deserves, and establish clearly the path or sequence the user should follow through the site. You will want to follow the same procedure when developing your signage.

Rely on thumbnails or miniature layouts as you go along. Keep working at this stage until you have a solution that seems to make sense. Roughs are not normally finished work, but are full-sized working models of the layout, with type and art in place. Roughs are close enough approximations of the completed project to show to clients to get the go-ahead. When you have an approved rough, you then arrange for production of camera-ready copy ready for film making or even direct-to-plate use.

The identity of team members and site selection should be determined and the instructor notified before you begin work. Both members of each team are equally responsible for handing in materials on time and in suitable form.

ASSIGNMENT AIDS   Following are two examples of how a tour might be arranged. Both examples utilize rudimentary maps. One of the examples calls out special features one by one and the other summarizes the features.

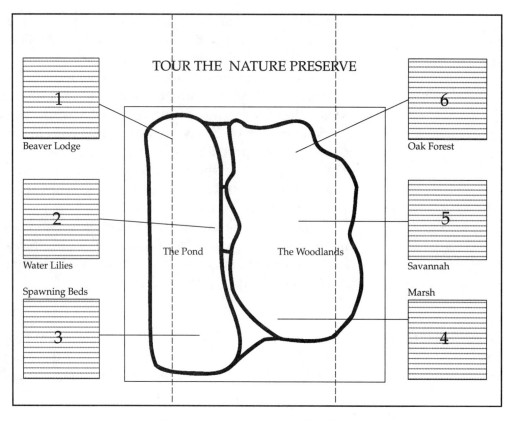

Three-panel brochure, with fold lines

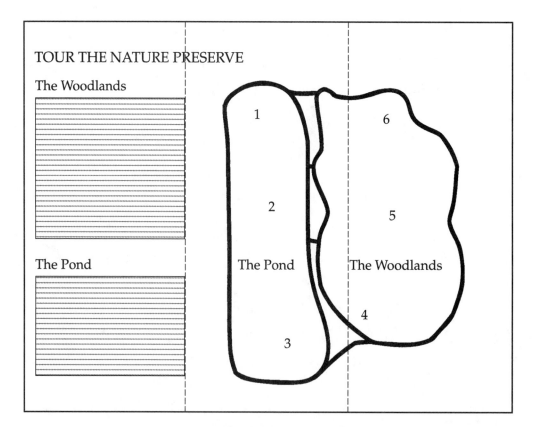

Three-panel brochure, with fold lines

18 NUMERALS

OBJECTIVE Although numerals that appear on printed material may not always register in a reader's consciousness, they are an important aspect of communication. For example, there is no more reader-friendly index-ing device in a printed work than a page number. Using numerals is a skill that should be mastered. Further, because we live in a world of numbers, the goal of readability of numerals can be as important in some contexts as the readability of text is in others. Numerals add not only information to graphic communications, but drama and beauty.

TO HAND IN Hand in a rough of a watch face and another of a clock face.

ASSIGNMENT
BACKGROUND Numbers have been an important part of the lives of human beings for many centuries, and they play an equally significant role today. Early on, women probably learned to count the lengths of their preg-nancies by the cycle of full moons. Men may have occupied them-selves trying to represent the numbers of animals in the herds they saw on the plains before them, and which they portrayed in beautiful colors on the walls of caves. Both men and women were probably keenly aware of the amount of time, again in the number of solar or lunar cycles, that crops needed from planting to harvest, as well as the number of fish that had to be dried if a family group was to survive a long winter. As soon as trading became a part of human existence and prosperity, numerals become even more important as they were ap-plied to keeping accurate accounts of things bought and sold. With the voyages of discovery and the need to accurately measure time and distances, and the discovery of regularities in nature, numbers became enshrined in the mind of humankind as revealers of the great mys-teries of existence. They helped human beings to see and describe more clearly their place in the universe. Eventually, it was mathemat-ics and numbers that helped humankind to learn to play the "music of the spheres."

Numbers are no less valuable or important today. People relate to them many times each day, and take them every bit as much for granted as they do the letters of the alphabet. We have seen that letter forms can be used expressively and we will now attempt to apply a ty-pography to numerals and learn to tease something out of their rich-ness and beauty.

Generally, numerals or figures may be differentiated in several ways. For starters, there are Roman numerals and Arabic numerals. Roman numerals are really capital-letter forms of the Latin alphabet letters I, V, X, L, C, and M. Arabic numerals are comprised of the curves and squiggles we all recognize. For Arabic numerals, typographers recognize modern and oldstyle forms, which are differentiated by their relationship to a baseline. The bottoms of modern figures all rest on the baseline, while oldstyle forms of the numerals 1, 2, and 0 rest on the baseline and rise to the mean line (so they are *x*-height); other numerals either have ascenders (6 and 8) or descenders (3, 4, 5, 7, and 9).

Generally, numerals need not stand out in a printed work any more than type does, and so it is often wise to select them from the same family and branch as the typeface they accompany, and in the same size. However, if the numerals appear to be too small when they are set in the same size as the accompanying type, a larger size may be indicated.

One use that everyone relates to from an early age are the numerals on watch dials or clock faces. It is in this context that they can be at their most expressive. From the time we turn over during the night to peek at the time (generally it's 2:30 A.M. or so), to the time when the alarm clock awakens us, to the end of the day and the 10 o'clock or 11 o'clock news programs, we are acutely aware of time. Most Americans wear watches, and if they don't, they are almost always within sight of a clock face. Frequent international travelers might even have watches with two faces on them, one telling the time of the place from which they departed, while the other shows the time at their destination. If one looks for them, watches and clocks can be found everywhere. In fact, they have become so ubiquitous and commonplace, as well as inexpensive, that the selection of a watch (and colorful band) has come to be just another fashion statement that anyone may make.

Because timepieces are so ubiquitous, we take them for granted, while at the same time holding them in high regard. Watches are often given to commemorate important events, such as the gold watch presented to a retiree or the gift at graduation, confirmation, or communion. Almost all families are aware of a watch or clock (often a grandfather-sized floorpiece) that has been in the family for oh so long, brought from the old country. There are also grandmother and mantel clocks, wall clocks, cuckoo clocks, regulators, and fun clocks (such as the cat clock, for which the tail serves as a pendulum and the eyeballs move back and forth in time). It is in this vein that this assignment is made.

ASSIGNMENT   The assignment is to design one watch face and one clock face using one or more of the numeral forms just discussed. You are expected to have at least all 12 numerals on the clock face. The watch face portion of the assignment is more wide open and has fewer restrictions; you may use as few as four numerals as well as any art you wish. As with any similar assignment, you will be well served by looking around and paying attention to the watch and clock faces you see each day. You may note that clock faces are a bit more functional and serious in tone than are watch faces, some of which might be classified as "fun." The watch face may be anything that strikes your fancy. Use your imagination to complete this assignment. Both watch and clock faces should be handed in at actual size, and the watch face should also be handed in enlarged four times.

19 RETAIL BAG

OBJECTIVE   This assignment allows you to exercise your imagination and go wild with art and type to create something both memorable and, perhaps, useful to a local merchant. You have the opportunity to bring together your knowledge of type and art to solve a common problem.

TO HAND IN   Hand in a full-sized finished layout of a bag such as those used by retail merchants.

ASSIGNMENT   Many retail merchants have come to see advantages to having their
BACKGROUND   logos and other promotional messages printed on the bags (sometimes called sacks or pokes) in which they pack up purchases for their customers. When it all works as it should, the customer becomes a walking advertisement for the merchant as he or she walks down the mall corridor. Some of the bags are quite well known. Tommy Hilfiger wants you to go forth with a well-stuffed bag emblazoned with his name, banner, and colors, as does Ralph Lauren. The Piggly Wiggly food chain has the happy little piggy face on its bags. Many food stores use seasonal designs, such as red holly berries and green leaves, on bags that can be used to wrap gifts at Christmas.

For the most part, these bags are not examples of high-quality printing. The paper or plastic used in their manufacture is minimally processed and is usually a variation on muddy white or brown. The paper is sturdy, but it is rougher than most printers can work with easily. In fact, a good many such bags are printed using the flexography process, which accommodates rougher surfaces and prints with inks that don't emit nasty odors, which would be a disaster in grocery store settings. The ink, while bold and colorful, doesn't rub off easily, which makes them appropriate for packing clothing. Plastic bags offer their own printing challenges. For the most part, photographs that depend on detail for their effect, extensive and smallish type blocks, fine lines, and the use of four-color process are out. Bold art, flat or spot color, and large and boldish type are in. Of course there are exceptions, and upscale stores tend to use higher quality papers, often colored and textured, to set off more sophisticated designs.

ASSIGNMENT   Design and produce a full-sized bag, sack, or poke for a retailer. If you wish to prepare a bag for a real store, look for one that suits your fancy in the Yellow Pages. If you wish, you may create an imaginary retailer or pick one that sells products of which you are especially fond. If you use an existing store, don't duplicate or copy their existing design, but make up a new look. Remember that there is a front to each bag and a back, which may have nothing printed on its surface. You can make this assignment look realistic by using a shopping bag and pasting or otherwise affixing your creative solution to it.

Use the following dimensions for your bag:

- If it is a paper bag, use 12 × 17, with handles.

- If it is a plastic bag, use 12 × 15, with handles.

20 POSTERS

Posters are ubiquitous. They appear in school hallways, corporate offices, libraries, and even tacked or stapled to utility poles. They speak to people as diverse as Americans, Mexicans, Parisians, Chinese, Russians, Indians, and South Africans. They range in size from a few inches wide and deep to larger than 24×36 inches. They may be entirely type copy, entirely visual copy, or a combination. This assignment allows you to exercise your imagination to develop a dramatic poster. For this effort, you must include visual copy.

TO HAND IN

- Four thumbnails of poster designs

- One rough, at least one-quarter size, of your best effort.

ASSIGNMENT BACKGROUND

Posters are a time-tested and time-honored medium for the expression of strong ideas. Posters have often been the medium of choice of members of minority groups, especially those who find themselves out of step in an authoritarian society. With mainstream media closed to critical or anti-establishment sentiments, posters can be an effective means of expressing the deeply felt emotions of minority members. They can be designed to be almost universal in their appeal, by stressing commonly understood emotions such as anger or despair and by treating familiar cultural symbols in powerful ways. They can be produced quickly with only a few simple production resources. They can be put up secretly by night to be seen by hundreds in a few minutes at dawn. They are often printed in color, which heightens their dramatic effect.

Posters are not entirely a modern phenomenon. They probably have been used to attract children—and children of all ages—to circuses for as long as there have been circuses. They had become a vehicle for serious commentary by the 1800s. For the most part, they are associated with two major human concerns: cultural and social conditions (including revolution) and commercial sales. They are strongly associated in the public mind with World Wars I and II. Viewed in retrospect, they are an art form as a well as an effective communication medium. Their form has been enriched from time to time by the attention of members of the more or less steady stream of art movements that have passed through the scene since the Art Nouveau-influenced posters of Toulouse-Lautrec.

Posters offer the advantage of being almost endlessly adaptable, to the point where it would not be a great reach to imagine highway billboards as big posters that have been appropriated to speak to people living in a car-based culture. On the other end of the size spectrum, a commemorative postage stamp might be considered a tiny poster, and graffiti on building walls and subway stations and cars might be thought of as poster-like art. It might not be such a stretch to identify as posters the newer "in-your-face" business cards that some aggressive souls have made their own.

No matter how they have evolved and been presented, the best known examples are associated with ideas strongly presented. There is no *ism* that has not spawned a poster program. Their creators have often been fiercely individualistic and talented, and the results of their work have been striking. The real test of their success tends to be in the streets, where they must, in a second or two, capture the attention of their intended audience and make their point. There is no second chance.

The characteristics of modern posters can be traced to Jules Cheret, who set up a color printing operation in Paris in 1866 and began to work on posters. He hit upon a poster formula that has stood the test of time: the best of them sell a benefit of an idea or a product, don't contain too much detail, and grab the viewer and make him or her a participant in the conspiracy. They can't afford to leave much to the imagination, and it goes without saying that size of type and brevity of message are crucial to their effectiveness. As one person put it, "A poster should be to the eye what a shouted demand is to the ear." Their large size shouts clearly.

Because Americans have so frequently been interested in both having and making their way, many of the more popular American efforts have been in the realms of war and of advertising. And because Americans have at least thought in grand terms of time and space (we have a lot of space), American posters tend to be a bit larger than European ones. A common size of American posters is 28 × 42 inches.

War has been an enduring subject for posters, and the major belligerents of World Wars I and II used posters to sell their citizens on the idea of supporting the war. Some have been memorable. Uncle Sam (he of the pointing finger) and Rosie the Riveter (she of the muscular, can-do persuasion) are familiar to most Americans. Although voluntary and enthusiastic service in the armed forces was a major theme of war posters, an equally important theme was the need for money. The cost of war might have bankrupted the governments of the world if new sources of capital had not been found. So, war bonds, and later voluntary relief, became poster themes designed to coax even pennies and nickels from the pockets of children. Experiences with war poster campaigns revealed how effective posters could be, and it was only a matter of time before posters were enlisted by advertisers to help create markets for a wide assortment of products and services ranging from cigarette papers, perfume, and automobiles to art openings and museum displays. As wealth increased, travel posters were used to encourage tourism. Many people have been so taken, at one time or another, by a particular poster, that they have framed it and displayed it prominently on the empty wall of home or apartment.

ASSIGNMENT   This assignment requires planning, preparing, and producing a poster. The subject is up to you. There are no constraints on content. It could be advertising, politics, or beauty of design for its own sake. Be thoughtful in your selection of art and type. After you have produced your thumbnails, discuss your favorite with the instructor and then work your best effort into a rough.

21 ADDRESS LABELS

OBJECTIVE
This assignment will challenge your creativity and exercise your developing talent for producing good typography and visual materials, as well as provide you ample opportunity for personal expression.

TO HAND IN
Hand in a rough of an address label for yourself, in actual size, and another enlarged to four times actual size. Use any colors and visual images you feel are appropriate.

ASSIGNMENT BACKGROUND
An address label is a product that few people really need, but it is also one that many feel they cannot do without. It may be difficult for younger people to believe that only 20 or so years ago most persons who addressed a letter also wrote their return address in the upper left corner of the envelope. This may have taken them a few extra seconds. But that was then, and this is now, and the world has apparently accelerated to the point where many letter writers no longer consider it a good use of their time to write their return address on envelopes. So address labels are sold, partly as a means to save time and energy. A second function they serve, and perhaps an even more important reason for their popularity, is that they offer people an opportunity to make a public statement about themselves, and at the same time enliven or jazz up their envelopes with attractive art and type.

It is easy to see that address labels must pack a good deal of graphic power into their small size if they are to be successful. As with most such convenience products, there are plenty of companies willing to provide a variety of choices wide enough to interest virtually anyone. In addition, insurance companies and charitable organizations frequently send along promotional address labels to customers, donors, and potential donors. For example, an insurance company might send along several sheets of labels with a holiday motif, accompanied by a letter urging policyholders to review their insurance needs in time for the new year; a veterans organization might use an American flag motif to point to their patriotic commitment and, by extension, the support of the person who affixes the label to his or her correspondence. The labels generally are self-adhering and backed on a roll or sheet. When you need a label, all you do is pull it off its backing and stick it on the envelope.

Companies that sell these address labels generally allow buyers to select a preferred style from a large number of examples. Sometimes buyers are allowed to mix and match to further personalize their labels. They may be permitted to select a personal monogram design rather than a visual symbol. There are offerings for designer labels, which integrate art and the address cleverly, at a slightly higher price. If you select a licensed image you usually pay extra for the privilege of having Snoopy pictured riding a mailbox-shaped airplane or Bugs Bunny peeking out of a hole in the ground next to a mailbox.

ASSIGNMENT   This assignment asks you to design and produce an address label for personal use. You will need to familiarize yourself with this product in order to understand the size to assign your label, typeface sizes, kinds of art in use, and so on. As you look around, you will see that most of most of them are not much wider than 2 inches, nor deeper than ¾ inch. There is no requirement that a label be rectangular, but remember that if you design an irregularly shaped one you might be faced with added costs to cover production of a die to be used to die-cut your unusually shaped label. Although it is possible you want a type-only label, develop a visual component to go along with the type for this assignment. This will allow you to make some basic decisions on integrating type and art in a small area.

Because a label is small, you might want to do your basic preparation in a size larger than the 2 × ¾ inch size of the final product, keeping in mind that you will ultimately have to reduce everything to the label size. This means that fine lines and intricate patterns may be lost in the reduction. Hand in an actual-size rough and one enlarged at least four times. Of course the roughs should be accompanied by your mark-up.

22 CHECKS AND CHECKBOOK COVER

OBJECTIVE This assignment will test your ability to attend to detail. It is also a good project for the exercise of your imagination. At the same time, you can't afford to abandon principles of good typography or fail to address special graphic-related requirements set by the nature of this particular type of communication.

TO HAND IN Hand in a rough of a check, as you would expect to find in a checkbook, as well as what is to be the front of your personal checkbook cover.

ASSIGNMENT BACKGROUND Who hasn't opened a checking account and as a part of the process ordered a batch of checks complete with checkbook cover? When you open a checking account, you are generally given a few checks to number by hand and use until permanent checks can be printed. The initial batch of 5 or 10 checks is usually best described as "dull, dull, dull." There is nothing distinctive about them; they are plain in typography and printed on nondescript paper. They have funny looking numerals along the bottom, set in a special typeface that can be read by an optical character recognition scanner and some smallish labels and lines here and there indicating where to place the name of the person to whom you're writing the check, the amount of the check, date, your signature, and so on. Although they accomplish what they need to, they are not the real you. You are a much more intriguing, even colorful, person. Check printers have recognized this and offer solutions. You can choose permanent checks that are not only acceptable to the financial community, but allow you make a personal statement about yourself, the real you, your inner self.

In fact, the hardest part of opening a checking account might be choosing the color and design of your personal checks. A week or so after you've made your selection, the checks arrive. You now have several hundred of them, a bunch of deposit slips, and other check-writing paraphernalia, ready to be inserted into the checkbook cover, which is usually a genuine plastic imitation of mammal, reptile, or amphibian skin. Perhaps your name is printed in gold ink on the front cover. Or, perhaps your initials in a swash type. You might have chosen a mythological creature to adorn the cover, such as a unicorn or griffin. Inside this dramatic cover, the checks are beautiful. Perhaps they portray a favorite cartoon character, a landscape, a racetrack, a space shuttle, or even space itself, with the moon and sun racing one another across the face of the check. They might portray just about anything. Of course your name, address and other information appear at the upper-left corner, and there are more of those funny-looking numerals along the bottom, which are machine-readable and serve to identify your financial institution and your account. They are numbered consecutively at the upper right. Now you can really start "hanging paper," beautiful paper.

ASSIGNMENT   Your assignment is to design a suitable check and checkbook cover that you feel represent you. Use any symbols you wish but remember that if you ordered, for example, a check with Mickey Mouse pictured on it, someone at the check company would have had to arrange for permission to use Mickey's features, and a small charge would likely be added to each check you use. As you begin work, think carefully about the proper dimensions for such a piece of paper larded with financial and legal requirements. You will want to take a close look at standard checks to learn what information commonly appears on their faces. Also pay attention to the typography.

When you have completed your research, begin work and follow it through to completion. Work on visualization and thumbnails and move along, when you're ready, to roughs. Complete the mark-up.

23 MONEY,
MONEY,
MONEY

OBJECTIVE   This assignment is really a current events assignment that will exercise your ability to use strong visual images, legible type, and numerals. It is a natural because the appearance of American money, both paper bills and coins, has been much in the news lately. There has, in fact, been a good amount of criticism of the newer designs of bills, as well as of the dollar coin. This assignment gives you an opportunity to participate in the discussion by providing design guidance to the Department of the Treasury. Draw on your experience with type, art, and the principles of design to complete this assignment.

TO HAND IN   Develop and hand in a design for the front and back of a paper bill of any denomination you choose for your empire.

ASSIGNMENT BACKGROUND   Aside from being an effective means for a person to exchange a piece of paper or a few metal coins for something that is much more appealing, such as a Popsicle, magazine, or bagful of tropical fish, money has an interesting past. We can be forgiven if we now tend to connect our money with dead white men. A good many former American presidents are pictured in classic poses on bills and coins. We have apparently grown used to this state of affairs and it is unlikely that our bills and coins will change much in the near future. But, as anyone who has traveled will tell you, Americans seem to settle for less imaginative and less attractive money than what is used or has been used in some other societies, even some that extend a good way into the past. For example, a number of Roman emperors used coins as a sort of news medium, wherein the person portrayed or the scene pictured on the face told citizens throughout the empire of new events or changes in the ruling force, alerting them to act accordingly. Current travelers often comment on the striking nature of money in the Netherlands, which is printed with beautiful and brilliant swatches of color. But when it comes to the U.S. approach to money, an old farmer overheard in a supermarket checkout line might have said it best, as he passed over one of the new $50 bills: "It looks like play money." Or Monopoly money or fancy coupons. But not real money.

ASSIGNMENT   However you feel about American money, this assignment will give you the chance to design a piece of paper money that meets your aesthetic needs. Rely for your inspiration on that old favorite dream of most of us: that we rule the world. So, the issuer of the bill is "The Yourname Empire." Design the front and back. You might want to begin by looking in your pocket to see, up close, what characteristics U.S. money displays and what size it is. For this assignment you will not have to worry about taking measures to thwart counterfeiters, but realize that most nations try to build such measures into their money, some by the clever use of typography and art. You may also freely decide upon the size of your bill (some nations print different denominations in different sizes). You should begin by learning what types of images and words tend to appear on money and what types of money are around. Do some visualization, move to thumbnails, and then get to the rough, which is to be handed in, marked up.

24 JUROR BADGE

OBJECTIVE You are to analyze this problem and provide a solution, with an emphasis on speed. You should be able to do three assignments of this nature before 9 A.M. every day of the week and four on the weekends. They are more pesky than profound, but there is no reason why a solution to such a problem should not be attractive as well as useful. Of course this type of assignment can be generalized to a number of alternative uses, including the need for identification materials for persons in corporate, educational, military, and other settings.

TO HAND IN Hand in a rough for a $3\frac{1}{2} \times 2\frac{1}{2}$ badge, to be worn on one's clothing.

ASSIGNMENT BACKGROUND Many American citizens are called each week to their county courthouses to meet their responsibilities as jurors. Persons ordered to report are generally checked in, given a short orientation to what is expected of them, or shown a video on the duties of jurors. Then some are selected to serve as prospective jurors for one case or another. Given the concern with security in courthouses and other public buildings, virtually all persons who work in such places are asked to wear some identifying symbol, often a badge, so their identity can be readily verified. When jurors are selected, they work in the courthouse, and they are often given identification badges to wear.

ASSIGNMENT This assignment is a simple one. Offer a design for such a badge, to be printed or copied in such quantities as are needed. The badge must clearly identify the person wearing it as a juror and must also identify the particular court in which the juror is serving. The printed portion of the badge will be inserted in a plastic holder that can be fastened or pinned to one's clothing. It should be simple and highly visible as well as easy to read. These requirements can be expected to bring into play selection of color and type as well as a consideration of good design principles. You can be as fancy or plain as you wish, although plainer and more straightforward seems better. This assignment begs for a businesslike approach, with little room for adding fancy or decorative material. Because so many of the jury selection chores are computerized, assume that the badge will be produced in quantity and names added by hand or computer printer as jurors are selected.

Information that must appear on the face of the badge includes:

- Juror

- Branch 1

- Winnebago County Circuit Court

- State of Wisconsin

Hand in a rough, marked up, with all required information carefully traced or printed by computer. You may print out the results on any color paper you think appropriate. You may also use any ornamentation you wish.

ASSIGNMENT AIDS   Here is an example of a juror identification badge.

Juror's badge

GLOSSARY

Accordion fold

A variety of fold characterized by a number of parallel folds, each successive one in the same direction, yielding a pleated effect. This type of fold works well when the graphic communicator feels that a particular message should, for effect, unfold for a viewer or reader. (Travel brochures and promotional brochures for vacation resorts might favor such a fold, which would allow the scene to unfold before the viewer's eye.)

Agate

A term that has several meanings. A named type size, 5½ points. Also refers to the small-type tabular material often found on sports pages, especially in the box scores. A measure of newspaper advertising, in particular national advertising, which was measured in agate lines (spaces one column wide and 5½ points deep).

Antique

A coarse or rough-surfaced paper, intended to appear to be made by hand.

Ascender

That part of a lower-case letter that extends above the mean line. Ascending letters include *b*, *d*, *f*, *h*, *k*, *l*, and *t*.

Author's alterations

In proofing, a change made to the copy by the author or client after it has been typeset. Typically, such corrections are charged to the author/client.

Backing

Printing a press sheet on both sides.

Baseline

A conceptual line on which the bottoms of characters in a typeface rest. Because all characters rest on this line, the type appears to be set in an orderly manner.

Basis size

A characteristic of paper. Each paper grade is produced in a particular and standardized size. If a graphic communicator can use paper in this size, it generally results in less waste in printing and hence, lower cost.

Basis weight

The weight, in pounds or grams, of 500 sheets of a grade of paper in its basic size. This measure provides for easy cross-grade comparison of papers and gives a graphic communicator a good indicator of the heft of a particular paper.

Binding

The process of fastening together press sheets on which the pages of a book or periodical have been printed.

Blackletter

A race of type. Blackletter is similar in appearance to the type first cast by Johann Gutenberg, which was imitative of the Germanic script drawn in and around Mainz in the mid-1400s.

Bleed

Art copy that extends through one or more page margins and off the edge of the trim page.

Blind embossing

Embossed material that is not printed with inks or covered with foil.

Blow-in

A small sheet of paper inserted, often by a puff of air, between pages of a periodical before it is mailed. Most blow-ins are self-addressed post-paid postcards that can be filled out and sent in by readers who wish to subscribe to the periodical.

Blurb

A short statement about the author of a book or periodical article, generally found on the inside back leaf of the cover or book jacket. Blurbs most frequently address the professional and intellectual qualifications of the author. A blurb can also be used to refer to a line on a magazine's cover intended to attract readers to articles inside.

Board

A grade of paper, popularly called *cardboard*, that is used primarily for packaging. A second important use of a board is in book binding, where stiff board is placed under the front and back covers of books. These boards protect the inside pages.

Body type

Type that is set en masse. Usually body type is the main carrier of the message. Body type can range from 6 points to about 14 points, although it is most often set in type that is between 9 and 12 points. Display types are larger than 14 points.

Boldface

A family branch. Boldface is heavier than normal type because the strokes comprising the characters are thicker. There are degrees of boldness, ranging from light, through demi-bold, bold and to extra- and ultra-bold. Normal type can also be called fullface or regular.

Bond

A grade of paper. Bond papers, commonly called *writing* or *ledger papers*, are primarily used in the office, for letterheads and correspondence as well as for invoices and other common business forms. The basic size of bond paper is 17 × 22, which can be efficiently cut to the common business size of 8½ × 11.

Book paper

A grade of paper. Book is the largest category of papers. Book papers are solid choices for virtually any printing need. The three categories of book papers are text, coated, and uncoated. The basic size of book paper is 25 × 38.

Brightness

A characteristic of paper. Brightness is a measure of how much light is reflected from a paper's surface. The brighter the paper, the more light is reflected and the higher the quality of the image printed is likely to be. Selection of a bright paper is extremely important for color printing.

Bulk/caliper

A characteristic of paper. Bulk is a measure of paper's thickness, expressed in either thousandths of an inch per sheet or, in the case of book publishing, in pages per inch. Generally, the bulkier the paper, the more serious and imposing the message it carries may appear. At the same time, the bulkier the paper, the more fiber it contains and the more expensive it will be.

Byline

The author's name that accompanies a news story or article. How it appears is a matter of style de-termined by each publication. Most appear at the beginning or at the end of an article.

Calender

The process of running paper between a series of rollers. The pressure of the rollers causes the paper to become smoother, thinner, and perhaps glossier.

Camera-ready

A pasted-up finished layout, called a *mechanical* or *comprehensive*, that is given to a camera person for filmmaking.

Cap line

An imaginary line to which all capital letters rise. All capitals rest on the baseline and rise to the cap line, which is often found a bit below the ascender line.

Capitals

Letter forms that are not lower case.

Caption

At one time this referred to a single-line title accompanying a piece of art copy. Captions often appeared at the top of the piece of art, and served to create a frame of reference for viewing the art. (For example, a humorous caption hinted to viewers that they should chuckle and not take the subject too seriously.) Over time, the word *caption* has come to be used interchangeably with the word *cutline*.

Case binding

The highest expression of the bookbinder's art. This traditional form of binding, also called *book binding*, *hard-binding,* or *edition binding*, requires assembling the signatures of the work, fastening them carefully, and sandwiching them between board for protection and durability.

Chroma

A measure of the intensity or brilliance of a color.

Chromalin proof

A color proof created from an assortment of dry powders.

CMYK

Abbreviation for the names of the ink colors used to print four-color process copy. The letters stand for, in order, cyan, magenta, yellow, and black. These colors are also referred to as *pigment primaries*.

Coated paper

A paper that is coated with a clay or other substance to improve one or more of its printing characteristics. Coatings range from dull and matte to very glossy (cast-coated).

Colophon

An identification mark, first developed by early printers. The most famed of them is probably that of Aldus Manutius, who used a dolphin and anchor to identify his work.

Column inch

A unit of measure used widely by newspapers. A column inch refers to a space one column wide and one inch deep. It can be used to refer to the size of an advertisement (for example a space two columns wide by four inches deep would contain eight column inches) or to the length of an article.

Compositor

A typesetter. Today, anyone active in desktop publishing is, in effect, a compositor, and all of the responsibilities of typesetting fall upon such a person.

Comprehensive

A finished, pasted-up layout, ready for filming. Also called a *mechanical*.

Condensed type

A family branch or variation of type in which characters seem to be squinched together. A full range of degree of condensation runs from condensed, through fullface, to expanded. In recent years, type designers have attempted to produce types that are both relatively condensed and readable in order to save space on the page.

Continuous tone

The name given to visual copy that appears to contain shades of gray. Black and white or color photographs are examples of continuous-tone copy. Actually, the continuous nature of the art is a trick played on the eyes by use of halftone dots, which makes the selection of the proper halftone screen, which contains the dots, an important decision for a graphic communicator.

Copy block

A block of type, usually referring to the copy in an advertisement.

Cover

A grade of paper specially constituted for use as cover paper for magazines. Cover-grade stock is manufactured to be durable enough to stand up to rough handling, as in mailing.

Crop/cropping

An editorial procedure that selectively removes portions of art copy, to remove irrelevant material or defects or to focus attention on important parts of the art.

Crop marks

Marks made on a piece of art to indicate to the person who will process the art copy what crop is desired, or what parts of the art should be removed. If one is using an actual print, or a negative, the marks are usually made in the border of the picture to protect the image.

CTP

Stands for "computer to plate," a prepress method that dispenses with the process of making film from which plates will be made. In CTP technology, the image to be printed is sent directly from the computer to the plate, and the plate can be placed directly onto a press, saving time and materials.

Cursive

A race of type imitative of handwriting. Generally, if individual characters appear not to be joined, the race is said to be cursive; if the characters appear to be connected, the race is said to be script. However, some typographers reverse these meanings or use the words interchangeably. Together, scripts and cursives comprise a race of type.

Cutline

The written explanations accompanying a photograph. Cutlines, sometimes called captions, answer viewers' questions about content of the photograph, including who is portrayed, when, where, and why. Cutline copy tends to be set in smaller type than text matter in the same publication, and perhaps in bolder type.

Cyan

A color of one of the process inks, used to print full-color art copy. The cyan plate is created when RGB colors green and blue are combined or added together. In appearance, this color looks like a variation of blue and is close to turquoise.

Dash

A printed mark, usually about one em in length, placed between words to create a separation in a reader's mind. This punctuation mark should not be confused with a hyphen, which is shorter in length and which serves to join words or create compound words.

Dateline

A line at the top of a news story that usually reveals when the news occurred and where. Given the pace of news today, the dateline has become virtually superfluous.

Deck

A portion of a headline. A deck often stands on its own, but does not necessarily tell the complete story of what occurred. Secondary or tertiary decks can add information for the reader. Many headlines today are multideck, the decks often differentiated by type size and family.

Deckle edge

A feathery edge on a piece of paper, created as paper fibers are formed at the edges of the paper-making machine wire. A deckle edge on a sheet lends an air of formality and elegance to whatever is printed on it. Very often, deckle edges are included on such printed materials as wedding invitations or announcements. A deckle also refers to the width of the roll of paper formed on a paper-making machine as well as to the wooden frame used when making paper by hand.

Decorative

A race of type, consisting of an often rather plain face to which a good deal of decoration has been added. A mental picture of such a face would be to imagine a capital *G* to which grape vines with bunches of grapes cling, in the midst of which can be glimpsed a cherub with wings, arrow, quiver, and a mischievous smile. Decorative types and novelty types are paired to form a single race.

Densitometer

An instrument used to measure reflected or transmitted light. Densitometers have a number of uses in printing, one of which is to measure whether the proper amount of ink is being laid on a piece of paper so as to produce a particular effect. Densitometers are also used to determine appropriate exposures for graphic arts film.

Descender

That part of a number of lower-case letters that extends below the baseline. Letters that have descenders include *f, g, j, p, q, y,* and *z.*

Desktop publishing

A means of creating periodicals and other materials on the computer. Desktop publishing programs provide for the creation of page elements and their movement on a page. In fact, desktop publishing is so easy that very little skill is needed to create page designs, which leads to a good deal of poor typography and poor design.

Didot point

A European type measurement, named for a famed printing family. The Didot point is a bit larger than the point adopted in the United States. There are approximately 67 Didot points in an inch.

Die-cutting

Using a metal form, much like a cookie cutter in concept, to cut or punch holes or windows in paper.

Digital typesetting

Typesetting by digital means. Digitized type is created by computers, which provides for easy control of type appearance.

Dingbat

An unusual symbol that often accompanies a font and is used for decoration or ornamentation or simply for typographic relief. Examples of dingbats include the symbols Œ, ∏, and .

Display type

Type sizes larger than body or text sizes. Generally, display sizes are 14 points and larger. Display types are meant to be seen rather than to be readable.

Dot gain

The tendency in printing for halftone dots to get larger as the run progresses. This is also called *dot spread.* The effect of changes in dot size and structure is that whatever is being printed becomes distorted to some extent and no longer true to the original. The effect can be especially pronounced when printing color.

DPI

Dots per inch. Used to identify the number of lines per inch on a halftone screen as well as the resolution power for the output of some printing devices.

Drop caps

Characters, usually enlarged and set in capitals, used to mark the beginning of paragraphs. These can also be called *initial letters.* The character used to create them is most often the first letter of the first word in the paragraph, and the enlargement is usually two, three, or four times the size of the body copy. Often these letters are inset into the paragraph although they might appear in the margin or rise above the copy block.

Dummy

Also called a *layout*. This is a model or a guide on which all elements that are to appear in the layout are accounted for (by position and size). A dummy is prepared partly for planning purposes and partly to guide others in preparing camera-ready copy. An alternative to creating a dummy is to make a comprehensive, which is camera-ready. However, relatively few persons have the technical ability to create quality comprehensives, so dummies are practical alternatives.

Duotone

Continuous tone copy that is printed in two colors. To achieve this result, two color negatives of the same image are produced by rotating a halftone screen to two positions, one for each negative. The two screened negatives are plated and each plate is printed in a different color, one usually in black and the other in the second color (two plates of the same color can also be used to achieve a similar effect). The effect is to enliven a halftone and give it bounce that it wouldn't otherwise have. If three negatives are made, the result is a tri-tone, if four, a quadratone.

Dylux proof

A commonly available proprietary proof made from a light-sensitive material. (Alternatives are called *brownlines*, *bluelines*, and so on.) After negatives have been stripped into a goldenrod, they are exposed on a sheet of sensitized paper. The image is made visible by the effect of the light and no further processing is required. The resulting proof is sent to the client or client's agent for correcting. Persons reading this type of proof should be focused on making certain that page elements are in place, right side up, that there are no visible defects and so on. If the dylux is perfect, the printer can move along to making a plate and printing.

Em

A measure of space related to the size of a particular font of type. An em is best conceptualized as an imaginary square space that is as wide as the typeface is high. Therefore, a 10-point em can be conceptualized as a space 10 points wide and 10 points deep. The em is an important measure in the graphic arts, as word-spacing and other type-related spacing is derived from it. For example, the normal amount of space between words is one-third of an em in width, although this amount of space is, confusingly, called a *three-em space*. This measure takes its name from the capital *M*, which in many typefaces requires a space that is just about square. At one time, typesetting charges were based on the em.

Em dash

A dash that is one em in length.

Emboss

A means of deforming paper in a controlled manner to create a raised surface that stands out from the paper ground. Embossing offers its user a rich and elegant effect. However, preparing to emboss paper can be a long and arduous process, requiring the making of two dies and the selection of paper that is of a suitable caliper or thickness. If the embossed design is not printed or covered with foil or treated in any special way, the embossing is said to be blind.

En

A space one half the width of an em. This measure takes its name from the capital *N*, which in many typefaces requires a space about half as wide as it is tall.

En dash

A dash one en in length.

End dash

The dash that was once used at the bottom of a news story in a newspaper. Its purpose was to signal the reader that the story had ended.

End mark

A mark placed at the end of the last line of a news story. Often a dingbat is chosen to signal the reader that the article is at an end; examples include □ and ■. *Newsweek* signals the end of its articles with a small black square, *Architectural Digest* uses the outline of a square, and *The New Yorker* uses a black diamond.

Engraving

An intaglio printing process that produces dramatic and beautiful results. The engraving process subtly distorts the surface of the paper and at the same time allows printing of extremely fine lines. The result is a richness of appearance.

Ephemera

If it is not a book and not a periodical, it likely falls into a category of printed material called *ephemera*. The label connotes a transient or non-continuing nature.

Expanded/extended

A family branch of type in which the type seems to be stretched horizontally along the line, making each character appear very wide or fat. The range of expansion runs from condensed through full face, to expanded and ultra-expanded.

Expert set

A type font that contains special characters used for particular purposes. For example, a font used in mathematical publishing would include such otherwise uncommon characters as subscripts and superscripts, Greek letters, and symbols used to indicate such operations as division and square roots of numbers.

Family

A group of type that displays particular characteristics in appearance. Such similar groups are given family names, including such useful families as Garamond, Bodoni, Futura, Baskerville, English Times, and Stymie. Families are, then, subsets of groups or races.

Family branch

Variations within a particular family. Common variations include degrees of expansion/extension, boldness, and posture.

Finish

A characteristic of paper. The finish or texture of paper can range from very smooth to quite rough. Selecting an appropriate finish for the paper a job will be printed on is important because paper can make an impression on readers when they pick up or touch a printed work. In addition, the paper's surface can affect printability. Common finishes are antique (rough), English (smooth), and eggshell (smooth).

Flat color

Another name for match or spot color. A graphic communicator can specify a particular color for any job by referring to a name or a number used in a color specifier system, such as Pantone. Such a system is analogous to the method familiar to interior designers of using paint chips to order particular paint colors at paint stores. The printer can formulate any color selected. There are a number of color systems in use in printing and it is imperative that both the orderer of printing and the printer are aware of the one in use.

Flexography

A type of relief printing resembling, in many respects, letterpress, except that the plate is rubber-like and flexible, and the ink is a water-based dye. Its advantages include its capability of printing on rough surfaces and the fact that its water-based ink leaves no hydrocarbon residue on the printed surface. The latter advantage makes it a good choice for food-related printing applications.

Floppy

The small memory storage devices commonly used in computers. Floppies have limited capacity and rarely find much use in heavy-duty graphic communication, where a single visual element in a layout might contain more information than a floppy is able to hold.

Folio

A single sheet of paper or, in book production, a page number.

Folio line

A line in a book or periodical that includes the page number. Sometimes the page number is accompanied by other matter, such as the name of the publication, date, and so on, in which case it might be called a *header* or a *footer*, depending upon where on the page it appears.

Font

An assortment of type from the same family branch and size. A font contains all of the characters needed to set type in that particular typeface and size. When metal type was used and type was sold by the pound, a font included an assortment of characters proportional to their use in the English language. In those days, when a typesetter did not have sufficient pieces of type to finish setting a work, the phrase "out of sorts" was used; of course this phrase now is used to express the state of one's health. As most type is now set using some kind of photographic or digital master, a proportional assortment of characters is not necessary.

Footer

Matter that appears at the bottom of each page of a book or periodical.

Formatting

Generally, refers to coding or giving instructions to a typesetting machine so that it sets type in the selected size, family, branch and font, with the desired spacing, line length, and so on, through all other meaningful variables. The word *format* is used to refer to the size and shape of a periodical.

Foundry type

Metal type with physical form, cast from molten metal in a type foundry. This kind of type was used from the days of Gutenberg until very recently. Setting metal type is now rarely undertaken commercially, although it might be used for fine arts purposes. Foundry type, if set and printed properly, can produce a finished product that is unrivaled in quality.

Fountain

A fountain is a trough on a printing press in which the ink is kept for distribution, by the aid of rollers, to the form or printing surface.

Four-color process

Full or realistic color printing of continuous-tone color copy. The decision to utilize four-color printing technology commits one to attempting to capture the reality of a moment on silver-based film and then trying to duplicate that reality in the printing process. Four-color printing attempts to create lifelike color using four particular inks. These process ink colors are cyan, magenta, yellow, and black (CMYK).

Galley proof

After copy is set into type, a galley proof is pulled of the typeset material and forwarded to the client or client's agent for correction. It is corrected or read for errors and returned to the typesetter, who makes the changes called for.

Gathering/collating

Generally, this is the process of bringing together the signatures of a book or periodical in proper order for binding. This is usually accomplished mechanically, on a binding line.

Goldenrod

An opaque sheet of paper or plastic film onto which film negatives are stripped prior to making a plate. The goldenrod is a mask for light and represents the printing surface.

Grain

A characteristic of paper. Grain is determined by the alignment of fibers used to make paper. As these cellulose or other fibers are formed into paper, they align disproportionately in one direction. Knowing the grain direction is important when determining how best to print and fold paper.

Grammage

A characteristic of paper. Grammage is a metric-based measure of the weight of paper.

Gravure

A printing process, also called *intaglio*. The image to be printed is formed below the surface of the printing plate. Ink fills the depression and a squeegee-like blade wipes off the excess; when the paper and ink come into contact, the ink is absorbed by the paper. Printing by use of this depressed surface means that the printing part of the plate never contacts paper or other substrate, and thus never wears as plates do in other processes; this allows long runs. Because of this property, and some others, its niche is printing long runs, with good detail of art and high-color fidelity on lower-quality paper. When the plate is rotary, the process is rotogravure.

Great primer

A named type size. Great primer was approximately 18 points. Other named sizes still used are agate (5½ points) and pica (12 points).

Gripper edge

The edge of a sheet of paper that goes through the press first. It is called the gripper edge because little metal fingers on the press cylinder catch onto or grip each sheet of paper to guide and pull it through the press. The gripper edge or gripper margin can become an issue for a graphic communicator because printing ink cannot be laid on the portion of the sheet held beneath the grippers. This may mean, for example, that a bleed photograph cannot be used on the gripper edge without making special accommodations. Printers can help graphic communicators to plan around such difficulties.

Grotesk

In Europe, sans serif type is called *grotesk* or *grot*. In the United States, the word *gothic* is often used, although the term *sans serif* is usually clearer.

Groundwood

Paper made from minimally processed cellulose fibers.

Group

In type identification schemes, synonymous with race.

Gutter margin

The inside margin of a page or middle margin of facing pages in a book or periodical. Although the gutter margin is typically the smallest margin on a page, having two of them on a spread of facing pages makes for a single rather large margin. Often, in magazine design, overcoming the separating effect of this large white area is a major problem. Sometimes the word *gutter* is used to identify the space between columns on a page, although the term *alley* might be more appropriate in this context.

H&J

Hyphenation and justification. When setting type, attention must be paid to these two variables or the copy can run out of control and the graphic communicator will be unhappy with its appearance. Often a computer program controls these variables, but in fine printing, decisions must sometimes be made line-by-line. One of the proofreader's chores is to "walk the lines" to check on hyphenation and justification.

Hairline rule

A rule or line that is very thin. Usually the width of rules is designated in points.

Halftone/halftone dots

As a continuous-tone image such as a photograph is readied for printing, it is screened. The screen breaks the continuous-tone image into dots of varying sizes and perhaps even varying sized dots in randomized positions. When these dots are printed, the dots create what the eye sees as the original continuous-tone image. The selection of the appropriate screen size and dot patterns and structure for a given continuous-tone image can often be profitably, and effectively, accomplished in coordination with a printer.

Hanging indention

A newspaper headline form that was at one time very popular. It is a three-line headline. The top line is long enough to span an entire column while two lines directly beneath it are equal in length to one another and both are indented an equal amount from the left margin. This form can be applied to textual matter.

Header

Matter that appears at the top of a page.

Highlight dot

A halftone dot that appears in the lighter areas of a printed halftone. Therefore, highlight dots are very small when printed.

Hue

A word used to identify a color. Simply stated, a hue is the name of the color and represents its place in the color spectrum. Of course, we are not very well equipped, given our language limitations, to identify more than a handful of colors. This makes the effective use of color a difficult enterprise.

Hyphen

A symbol used to tie together language elements. In its simplest form, it is used to create compound words. It is also used to break words into syllables at the end of lines of type.

Imposition

The arrangement of pages on a press sheet so that when the sheet is printed and folded into a signature, the pages appear in the proper order. Printers can help graphic communicators determine which imposition will best meet particular needs and help them to understand the consequences of using one imposition scheme over another.

Indention

Not indentation. This is the space the first line of a new paragraph is inset from the left margin. Such insets efficiently alert readers that a new paragraph is beginning. Commonly, the amount of indention is described in terms of ems.

Initial letter

The first character in the first line of a copy block that is larger than the rest of the type in the block. The functions of an initial letter include attracting attention and serving a step-down function for the reader's eye as he or she moves from display type size in a headline to body type size.

Ink jet

A means of plateless printing in which ink is broken into fine droplets and sprayed through tiny jets onto a surface. Because the jets can be controlled by computers, ink jet printing is a convenient means of creating publication address labels or personalizing otherwise identical messages sent to large numbers of people.

Inline letter

A letterform in which there is a white or blank area within the stem strokes of a number of characters.

Intaglio printing

See Gravure printing.

Italic

At one time italic was a separate race or group of type, although it now refers to any typeface that is tipped or inclined to the right.

Jim dash

Once a name given to a dash used to separate decks of a headline.

Justified type

Type set en masse so the left and right margins are parallel. Currently, it is the most common column arrangement for type, although its use may present spacing, hyphenation, and justification problems. It is still the favored columnar arrangement for setting news copy.

Kerning

A letterspacing arrangement in which space between particular letter pairs is removed. In kerning, the amount of space removed varies according to the letter pairs. Kerning often improves the appearance and readability of type.

Keyline layout

A layout on which instructions for the proper assembly and placement of elements are given on an overlay sheet.

Keyline proof

Generally, a color proof composed of layers of film, one layer each for yellow, magenta, cyan, and black. Because the color layers are transparent, when they are viewed one atop another, in register, they closely represent how the work will appear when it is printed.

Kicker

A form of newspaper headline. The kicker line appears above the main headline and gives the headline writer an opportunity to add information that provides a framework for interpreting the material. Kicker lines are set in smaller type than the main deck and are often underlined. A reverse kicker or hammer has a word or two in large type above the main headline deck, which is set in smaller type.

Laid paper

Paper that is handmade or machine-made paper that includes visible characteristics that (falsely) hint that it is handmade. The telltale pattern of handmade or laid paper, visible when a sheet is held up to the light, is that of parallel lines running almost in a ladder shape across the sheet. The lines mimic those that appear on handmade paper, and thus indicate quality. The marks can be created on a papermaking machine in much the same way watermarks are created.

Leading

Spacing between lines of type, usually indicated in points, and often amounting to only a point or two. Adding even such small amounts of space tends to increase readability.

Ledger paper

A special kind of bond paper that was once used primarily for accounting purposes, where erasing was common. Ledger paper has a good deal of surface strength and resists abrasion.

Legibility

The visibility of type. Type that is legible tends to "jump off the page" into the reader's eye. This term is sometimes used interchangeably with *readability* but should not be so confused. Legibility is seeability; readability is a measure of comprehension over time of material set in type.

Letterpress

A printing process that prints by means of a raised or relief surface. The part of the plate that is raised receives ink which is then transferred, by pressure, onto paper or substrate. Letterpress creates a debossed printing surface, and when the paper used has a rougher surface, the effect can be extremely rich, adding the dimension of quality to a job. Commercial printing by letterpress is not common, although a number of finishing operations, including die cutting, foil stamping, and numbering utilize letterpress presses.

Letterspacing

Space between individual characters. Although all characters have space designed into them so they don't touch other characters, letterspacing usually refers to adding additional space or removing what is already there. This manipulation of space is usually done to increase readability or save space. When the same amount of space is added or taken from between each letter, it is called *tracking*; when varying amounts of space are removed, it is called *kerning*.

Ligature

Occurs when two or more characters are visibly joined. At one time, ligatures were intended to protect parts of some characters from breaking off when printed. Tying the characters together into a ligature strengthened the weakness in one and made both characters more resistant to breaking. The use of ligatures today has no such practical use, but is usually an affectation. Examples of ligatures include æ and fl.

Line art

Art or visual copy that consists only of solid black lines. There are no continuous tones on line art, although the effect of grays can be created by use of crosshatch marks or other texturing methods.

Line conversion

A dramatic presentation of a continuous-tone halftone. In this technique, the original continuous-tone copy is not screened, so the image is not broken into dots as in a normal halftone film. Portions of the original image that reflect about 40 percent or less light do not record on the film, while portions that reflect more than about 40 percent record as black. Thus, rather than continuous tones, the image is converted to a dramatic black and white form. This is a very helpful technique when the desire is to present strong images, especially if the subject has strongly vertical or horizontal aspects.

Logotype
An identifying mark. At one time, this referred to a metal type body cast with more than one element on it. It now refers, loosely, to any identifying mark, from a brand mark to a corporate mark to the flag or nameplate of a newspaper.

Lower case
Small letters of the alphabet, or minuscules, as opposed to upper-case or capital letters.

Magenta
One of the four-color process colors. Magenta appears more maroon than red.

Majuscule
Another word for upper-case or capital letters.

Mark up
The process of communicating to a typesetter how typeset copy should appear. Marking up copy typically addresses such matters as type family, family branch, type size, leading, line length, indention, and so on.

Master pages
In a number of composition programs, users may insert page constants on these representative pages (left and right) and the constants will then appear on individual pages throughout the publication, on right and left pages, respectively. Folio lines are commonly placed on master pages, and then the appropriate page numbers appear on all pages in the publication. Constants thus placed can include type copy as well as art or visual copy.

Match proof
A high-quality, and expensive, color proof. The benefit of ordering a match proof is accurate color rendition. That is, the colors as they appear on the proof will be identical to those that will appear on the printed work.

Mechanical binding
A catch-all category of binding, including loose leaf, spiral bound, plastic comb, and so on. Generally, these binding forms are cheap, and they look neat and orderly.

Mortise
A mortise involves removal of a part of a halftone. Type copy or art or visual copy can be placed in the hole. This technique is a natural if one wishes to dramatically show relationships. The terms *notch* and *mortise* have become used almost interchangeably, although originally a mortise was visualized as a hole in a halftone surrounded completely by halftone copy, while a notch involved removing a portion of a halftone, including at least one edge of the halftone.

Notch
See Mortise. When part of continuous-tone copy is removed, and when the portion removed touches an edge of the halftone copy, it is called a notch.

Novelty
A race of type. Generally, novelty typefaces are designed to fulfill a special purpose or to reinforce, typographically, the content of an idea. For example, a typeface with Cyrillic-appearing letterforms substituted for Latin letterforms would be a natural on a poster announcing a lecture by a Russian novelist. A typeface that mimicked stenciled letters would be a good choice for an import-export company advertisement. Often, decorative types and novelty types are combined to create a single race.

Numerals
Numbers or figures. There are several choices of how numerals will appear. Roman numerals can be upper case or lower case, and Arabic numerals can be lining (the bottoms of all figures are strung along a baseline) or oldstyle (some numbers have parts extending below the baseline).

Optical character recognition (OCR)
This capability allows for machine recognition of alphabet characters, numerals, and punctuation. Use of a scanner with OCR capabilities can save a good deal of the time often required to input a manuscript.

Oblique
Used interchangeably, if erroneously, as a synonym for *italic*. Oblique type slants to the right, and the degree of incline can often be controlled in the typesetting process by digitally or optically distorting the type. Italic type was at one time a separate race, designed in the inclined form.

Optical center
One of the more important locations on a page. It is the place to which a reader's eye is attracted, all

other things being equal. It offers an opportunity for a graphic communicator to emphasize the most important part of the message, simply by placing it on the optical center. The optical center of a page is about 60 percent of the distance up from the bottom of the sheet, and, at least in Western culture, slightly to the left of the vertical centerline.

Offset lithography/Photo-offset lithography

A printing process. This process prints from a flat or planographic surface, prepared by making it differentially receptive to ink (the ink adheres only to the portion of the layout that is to print). It is currently the most popular and most available printing process. Because the printed image is offset onto a slightly flexible, rubberlike cylinder, the image can ultimately be transferred onto paper that is slightly rough (and therefore probably cheaper than more highly processed stock). This process has, therefore, been a natural for taking advantage of the interest of newspaper readers in visual journalism; good quality photographs can be reproduced on relatively cheap newsprint.

Opacity

A characteristic of paper. Paper characterized by a high degree of opacity can be printed on both sides without show through. Opacity is therefore an important characteristic if printed materials are to be backed, that is, printed on both sides of a sheet of paper.

Orphan

An orphan occurs when about one-third of a line of type or less appears as the last line in a column of type.

Outline halftone

A halftone in which the background has been dropped out, leaving only the figure the designer wishes to emphasize in silhouette. This is a useful technique for focusing viewers' attention on the subject pictured.

Outline letter

A family branch or variation of a typeface in which the letter is outlined, with inside portions not filled in.

Overlay

A transparent sheet fastened in place over a layout. Such a sheet provides both protection for the layout beneath and a place for a graphic communicator to make special notes for the person who will next work on the layout.

Overset

Copy set into type but which cannot be used in the final version of the printed material because of lack of space. Overset is expensive. A graphic communicator who knows how to apply copyfitting procedures can reduce the amount of overset in a job by carefully estimating how much will be needed before copy is generated.

Page constants

Printed matter that appears on virtually every page of a book or periodical. A folio line is an example of a page constant, as is a magazine logotype, if it appears on all pages.

Page proof

A proof of a page, as it will appear when printed, with all page elements that will appear on that page in their proper locations.

Pagination

Area composition. Pagination provides for the electronic assembly of graphic elements into pages. When a page has been so assembled, it can be sent in complete form for filming or even directly to the press.

Pantone Matching System

One of the more widely used color identification systems. The Pantone system resembles a paint swatch booklet, allowing a graphic communicator to select a specific color from among hundreds. The system also provides a formulary so a printer can mix inks to produce the identified color.

Parallel fold

A fold that runs in the same direction as a previous fold. A right-angle fold runs perpendicular to a previous fold.

Paste-up

The process of physically assembling page elements on a dummy sheet. The paste-up artist brings together type and art copy into a finished form, ready for filming. Physical paste-up of page elements is rarely done these days. Almost all makeup or area composition is done on computers.

Perfect binding

A form of binding that relies on an adhesive to hold pages or signatures of a publication together. Perfect binding is relatively cheap and permits binding virtually limitless numbers of pages. Most paperback books and telephone directories are perfect bound.

Perfecting press

A press that prints both sides of a sheet or roll of paper on a single pass.

Phototypesetting

Typesetting that uses light projected through a lens system and a template onto photosensitive paper to create type that is ready for paste-up after development.

Pica

A measure used in the graphic arts. A pica is 12 points.

Planographic printing (See Offset)

Printing accomplished by means of a flat surface.

Point

A measure used in the graphic arts. A point is 1/72 inch.

Posterization

A dramatic treatment for halftones in which the number of tones in a piece of continuous- tone copy is reduced to three or more instead of having a virtually limitless number of shades of gray.

Posture

The orientation of a family branch of type to the vertical. Postures can be perpendicular or italic or oblique.

Printer's errors/PEs

When typeset copy is proofed, the errors in the typeset copy that can be attributed to the typesetter's carelessness are called printer's errors. The cost of correcting printer's errors is borne by the typesetter, if they are noticed by the proofreader.

Process color

Another word to indicate four-color process.

Proofreading/Proofing

The process of correcting typeset or visual material so it conforms to what was sent out for typesetting or filming, and what is desired when it is in finished form. Proofreading is perhaps the most important task a graphic communicator is asked to undertake. If mistakes are not caught by a proofreader, they will likely appear in the printed material and could be embarrassing. There are a number of proofs commonly pulled at points in the preparation and printing stages, from galleys to page proofs.

Quad

A measure of space, synonymous with em, a square of the type size.

Quire

One-twenty-fifth of a ream of paper, or 40 sheets.

RGB

Red, green, and blue, the three light primaries. These are additive colors, and by adding varying proportions of them in combination, all of the colors of nature can be reproduced. They are related to CMYK, for example, because combining red and blue produces magenta, green and blue produce cyan, and red and green produce yellow. When the pigment primaries are printed, they can mimic closely the colors of nature.

Race

Type is divided into a number of races. Races differ in appearance. Placing families in races recognizes gross differences in type appearance. A typical listing of races would include blackletter, Roman oldstyle, Roman modern, Roman transitional, sans serif, square serif, cursive/script, and decorative/novelty.

Ragged left

Type that is justified on the right but allowed to range on the left. This form of presentation is not usually highly readable.

Ragged right

Type that is justified on the left but allowed to range on the right. This form of presentation promotes readability because it allows for natural letter and word spacing and requires fewer word breaks and hyphens or unusual spacing arrangements.

Rainbow proof

A proof, much like a match proof in function, but cheaper.

Readability

A measure of how easily typeset material can be read.

Ream

Five hundred sheets of paper constitute a ream.

Recto

Another name, if antiquated, for a right-hand page in a book.

Register

When a press is able to print an image time after time in the same position it is holding register. Register is an important concept when printing two or more colors in the proper relationship with one another throughout a run.

Relief printing
Generally, printing from a raised surface, which could be anything from a rubber stamp to letterpress printing.

Reverse surprint
White type on the face of a continuous-tone copy.

Revised proof/revise
After a galley is proofread and sent back to the typesetter for correction, the resulting corrected proof, when pulled, is a revise.

Right-angle fold
A fold that is made at right angles to another. A right angle fold contrasts with a parallel fold.

Roman modern
One of the major races of type, characterized by a pronounced vertical angle of stress, very thin or hairline serifs, and a good deal of variation between thick and thin strokes that make up each character in a font. The archetypal modern is Bodoni.

Roman oldstyle
One of the major races of type, characterized by an inclined angle of stress, bracketed serifs, and little variation between thick and thin strokes that make up each character in a font. The archetypal oldstyle is Garamond.

Roman transitional
One of the major races of type, characterized by angles of stress, serifs, and variation in stroke thickness that are somewhere between modern and oldstyle. The archetypal transitional is Baskerville.

Rotogravure
Gravure printing from a cylinder. Extremely fast printing can be accomplished on lower-quality paper.

Rough
Although this is a relative term (one person's rough may not be rough at all), it is generally understood to be a layout that, while not completed or camera-ready, is sufficiently complete to allow a client to examine it and to give final approval.

Rule
Any line printed on a surface. Generally, rules are measured in points of thickness. Special decorative rules are usually given names, such as a Scotch rule.

Run
Printer's term referring to a job that is to be printed. "What is the run?" would be understood as "How many copies of this job are we printing?"

Runaround
Type contoured to an irregular shape, such as an outline, silhouette halftone, or other piece of visual copy.

Running matter
Material that appears continually through a publication, as in a periodical. A columnist's logo that appeared regularly would be called running matter, as would a masthead. The most common running matter might be a magazine's logo and page number on each page.

Saddle stitch
A form of binding in which the folded signatures are gathered by placing one atop another, in a manner resembling a saddle. A wire staple is then driven through the signatures to create a bound publication, which is trimmed and readied for distribution.

Sans serif
One of the major races of type. As its name indicates, there are no serifs on such type, and it is very likely that all strokes that make up a character are uniform in thickness.

Score
The process of bringing a scoring rule down on a sheet of paper hard enough to compress paper fibers along the rule line. Later, when the sheet is folded, the fold is easier to accomplish because of the pretreatment.

Screen printing
A printing process using a stencil. The ink oozes through the open areas of the stencil and is held back by the impervious portion of the stencil.

Script
One of the major races of type, often paired with cursive in a single race. Type in this race is imitative of handwriting and so can project a formal and informal character simultaneously. Typically, if the characters appear to be joined, they are called *script*, and if there are small gaps between them, they are *cursives*. Sometimes this definition is reversed.

Self-cover

When a periodical or piece of ephemera has a cover printed on the same stock as the pages inside, it is said to have a self-cover. Many periodicals, especially those mailed to subscribers, rely on a separate cover, printed on a stock that is more durable or has other favorable characteristics suitable for mail and newsstand distribution.

Separate cover

See Self-cover. When the cover of a periodical is printed on a different stock than the inside, it is said to have a separate cover.

Separation

The entire set of four pieces of film, produced as an intermediate step if one desires to print material in four colors. By using a filter of one type or another (optical or digital), the film house or color separator produces a piece of film that produces a plate that prints each of the process colors, yellow, magenta, cyan, or black.

Series

This term, more closely associated with metal type, refers to the array of sizes in which a given type was produced. This term is no longer used, given photo and digital typesetting, as lenses and computers can produce an array of sizes using the same template or digitized instructions.

Serif

The small finishing or ending strokes on stems of characters in roman and square serif types.

Set

Refers to how much width on a line a type requires when set. A typeface that takes up a good deal of space "sets wide."

Shaded letter

A family branch in which characters appear to have shadows.

Shadow dot

A halftone dot that appears in the darker areas of a printed halftone. Therefore, shadow dots are large in size.

Sheet-fed press

A press that prints on sheets of paper rather than on rolls (see Web-fed).

Sidewire stitch

A form of binding that has been superseded largely by perfect binding. In sidewire, signatures are assembled by stacking them atop one another and driving a wire staple through them at the edge of the fold.

Signature

A press sheet for a multipage job that has already been printed and folded. The imposition guarantees the pages will appear in the proper order after folding. The printer should be consulted to learn about the arrangement of pages on a press sheet and to discuss the consequences of this arrangement.

Silhouette halftone

An outline halftone. A halftone in which the dots have been removed from all but the subject, as selected by the graphic communicator. This is a very popular halftone form given the ease with which background dots can be removed digitally.

Small capitals

Capital letter forms that are no higher than the x-height of the face.

Sorts

An antiquated term referring to the small metal pieces of type. Setting type (in English) requires an assortment of types with more *E*s than *Q*s and so on. When a printer ran out of one of the characters (a possibility when setting a big job), he or she was said to be "out of sorts." This phrase is now used to indicate a physical state of a person who is not "up to par."

Split-fountain

The fountain of a press is the tray that holds the ink. In some instances, a fountain can be split or separated so that ink of two colors can be printed by the same press unit from the single separated or otherwise divided fountain.

Spot color

Another name for flat color. Generally, spot color is a precise color that is required by a graphic communicator. No other color will do. In such cases, the graphic communicator must communicate to the printer precisely the color needed. Generally, a system such as the Pantone Matching System is used to accomplish this.

Square Serif

One of the races of type. Characters in this race or group generally have little stroke thickness variation, but have serifs that are about the same weight as the strokes themselves. This race appears, therefore, to be blocky or stocky.

Straight matter

Body type uncomplicated by anything more than paragraphing. There is no tabular matter and no need to arrange type specially. Consequently, type compositors charge less for type set in this configuration.

Surprint

Type of any color printed on the face of continuous-tone copy. If the type appears as white, it is said to be a *reverse surprint*. These are combinations of type and continuous tone copy.

Swash

A decoration on some letters in some fonts. When part of a letter is continued below the baseline in a flourish, that is a swash. This affectation often appears on signage. Good letters for swashing are *G*s, *F*s, and *Y*s. A good rule for using swash letters is "Use one if you wish, but never more than once every five or ten years."

Text paper

A type of book paper of outstanding quality.

Thermography

Faked engraving. A printing process, more exactly a finishing process, in which a resin that adheres to printed material is applied and later melted by being exposed to heat. This produces a raised surface. It is a 3-D process that adds depth to what is printed.

Thumbnail

A small version of a layout. This is a necessary start to the preparation a graphic communicator makes as he or she commits ideas, through words and art, to paper. Because these are small and take little in the way of preparation, thumbnails can be produced in quantity to allow assessment of a wide variety of possibilities before proceeding toward a more finished rough stage.

Tint block

A gray background for type or continuous tone. The gray results from printing black or other colored dots at a specific percentage of gray and then printing black type over it.

Tip-in

A means of adding pages, or even a separate publication, to a bound periodical. The additional material is printed and trimmed separately and then glued into place in the binding process where it becomes a part of the finished work. Although tipping in pages increases the price of production, it can allow users of the material to tear it from the publication for future reference and use.

Tracking

The addition of a set amount of white space between all characters in typeset copy. Tracking can be normal, negative, or positive. The amount of space added or subtracted is small and is generally referred to in terms of units.

Trim marks

Marks printed on a press sheet to indicate where trimming to finished size is accomplished. These marks are printed, but because they appear outside of the finished area, they are trimmed off and never appear on the final version.

Trimming

The process of cutting a work to its finished size.

Type policy

A complete list of all typographic choices that a graphic communicator thinks is necessary to communicate the message effectively. A comprehensive list of all the possible ways type is to appear in a printed work.

Upper case

Capital letter forms.

Value

A describer of color, a part of the vocabulary of color. A color's value is its relationship to gray; for example, adding black to green produces a dark green, while adding white produces light green. The dark and light are values.

Vellum

Prepared animal skin, usually sheep or goat, on which early scribes recorded written works. Now it refers to a type of paper that is treated to imitate animal skin. Vellum feels smooth and appears to have an inner glow, which can be very attractive.

Verso

Another name for a left-hand, or even-numbered, page.

Vignette halftone

Fading at the edges of the dots of a halftone. This was a popular technique of early photographers who worked on portraits of women and children. It reached its popularity peak in the earlier 1900s.

Web-fed press

A press designed to print on a roll of paper. A web-perfecting press would print on both sides of a roll.

Whiteness

A characteristic of paper. This is a measure of its relation to pure white, and therefore this variable assumes importance in the printing of color, when using a paper of any color other than white might affect the nature of the reflected color.

Widow

Less than one half of a line of type that appears at the top of a column of type. An editor tries to rid copy of such defects.

Wordspacing

The amount of space placed between words. Unless otherwise indicated, this space will be a 3-em space (which is actually one-third of an em).

Wrap

A binding technique that allows additional material to be included with a periodical. In this method, one or more sheets, folded, are inserted around a signature and then bound into the periodical.

x-height

The height of a lower-case x. This measurement defines the portion of the background grid on which characters are formed that lies between the baseline and the mean line.